TOP PRODUCER
SECRETS

CONFIDENTIAL

TOP PRODUCER
SECRETS

A New Way of Selling for New Home Sales Professionals

Shirleen Von Hoffmann

authorHOUSE®

AuthorHouse™
1663 Liberty Drive
Bloomington, IN 47403
www.authorhouse.com
Phone: 1-800-839-8640

First published by AuthorHouse   4/1/2010

ISBN: 978-1-4490-7928-4 (sc)
ISBN: 978-1-4490-7930-7 (e)
ISBN: 978-1-4490-7929-1 (hc)

Library of Congress Control Number: 2010904037

Printed in the United States of America
Bloomington, Indiana

This book is printed on acid-free paper.

What people are saying about
"TOP PRODUCER SECRETS"

"This book will change the way you sell. Shirleen's common sense approach will guarantee your sales success. The material in this book captures the essence of how to get to the top. It's a must read for sales professionals".
Jerry Rouleau
Selling More Homes Media & J. Rouleau & Assoc.

"Shirleen, Congratulations on creating a valuable educational treatise and resource for anyone wanting to learn how to become a more effective and successful new home salesperson in today's challenging market".
S. Robert August
PRESIDENT, BA, MIM, NAHB Life Director, Fellow, MIRM, CMP, CSP, MCSP, CAASH

"This book is full of great ideas and is "back to basics" of sales. It reminds our Sales People of what they need to be doing in this market. I know it works because Shirleen trains my team and they are the best! We get fantastic results from her training and simple sales wisdom."
Jill Hardy Vice President Regis Homes
Northern California

"I have read a number of books on the subject of new home sales and most of them seemed to be based on theory. I loved how this book was different, more practical and hands on with takeaways for the Agents. You want an edge on the competition, look no further."
Dave McKown
Director of Sales and Marketing
William Lyon Homes

"Ms. Von Hoffmann's book, "Top Producers Secrets" offers terrific insight and roadmaps to success for all sales agents in the new era of the "New Normal."

This book is a must read not only for all new home sales agents and their management teams but any builder looking to survive and get the "Edge" during the next decade."
Bill Heartman
President
Regis Homes Northern California

"I have been a Sales Agent for 20 years and I love this book. I think this book should be in the hands of every Sales Agent in the country. This book is loaded with great ideas and knowledge with takeaways done in small steps. It is easy and something everyone can learn from! Great Job!"
Renicia Fewell, New Home Sales Person & Broker

"Shirleen Von Hoffman's **"Top Producer Secrets",** tells it like it is when she describes her Blueprint for Success; it doesn't happen by accident. Whether you're a builder, sales manager or sales agent, Shirleen provides not only a theoretical blueprint for success but the step-by-step process to make it happen!" I really enjoyed reading this book!
Zoe Miller, Owner
Computer Presentation Systems

Foreword:

Shirleen Von Hoffmann, better known as "The Queen of Sales" is a Sales Coach, Broker, Business Owner, Author, Inspirational Speaker and expert in Sales and Customer Service Excellence.

Shirleen says, "During my 28 year career in New Home Sales, the one constant thing I noticed missing, no matter who I worked for, was the lack of support, training and understanding of Sales People and what they encounter day in and day out. If I wanted great training, it didn't come from my Managers or companies, I had to seek it out and pay for it myself.

It always bothered me that Real Estate Sales People didn't get the training and support they needed, especially because they are the closest contacts to the customer. After many years as a Top Producing Sales Person and Manager I knew that my later-life career needed to be dedicated to supporting Sales People, Sales Managers and the companies who hire them.

At Home Builders AdvantEdge we focus on exceptional sales coaching, consult, video and written employee performance evaluations and "VIP" customer service training for Home Builders and their Sales People. It is my hope that this book will make a significant impact on your sales and will improve your business for many years to come."

Shirleen Von Hoffmann, President

Home Builders AdvantEdge

Our Purpose - is to support Builders and their Sales Teams, in their quest for excellence. Through our EDGE Program of sales training, coaching and consulting, we bring a "new way" of thinking, selling and marketing new homes.

Our Goal – is to enlighten Builders to their challenges and find solutions as well as train their Sales Professionals to be the best they can be; "EDGE Agents".

Our Value – is to make a positive difference in their lives; increased sales potential; peace of mind and a more prosperous bottom line.

Our Mission – is to help Builders and Sales Professionals develop their skills and move them to a fresh place of success they have never experienced before.

The skills we teach will not only make New Home Agents more "in control" and thorough in the sales process, but more in control of their individual destinies as well. If you follow our curriculum you will have the very best Sales Teams in the business.

We are not typical sales trainers. We teach a specifically designed curriculum, in a way Sales Agents can grasp, in a new home language they understand. This training will change the roles and skills of New Home Professionals making them successful in all markets.

This book is dedicated to all the New Home Professionals in the world. From Sales People and Builders, to Managers, Superintendents, Land Acquirers, Warranty, Title, Escrow Representatives Lenders and even the state agencies who govern us.

We are all one family with one common interest and goal. We have the immense honor and responsibility of developing thriving communities in our nation with happy families that live in our homes.

There is no better way to make a living!

Thanks so much to my Sales Teams who inspire me and the Builders I learn from every day and who have always challenged me to do my very best. Over the years I consider you all my dear friends.

Thanks also to all my "Real Estate" sales girlfriends who are my advisors as well. Cynthia Sharp and Renicia Fewell thanks for all your help ladies!

To my editor Anne Murphy, thank you so much for your second set of eyes and helpful suggestions. You have no idea how much I appreciate your effort.

Many Blessings!

Shirleen

TABLE OF CONTENTS

CHAPTER 1: WHO IS A TOP PRODUCER?   1
CHAPTER 2: BECOME AN "EDGE AGENT"   7
CHAPTER 3: SECRET #1   19
SECRET #2   25
SECRET #3   35
SECRET #4   47
SECRET #5   53
SECRET #6   57
SECRET #7   69
SECRET #8   77
SECRET #9   85
SECRET #10   93
SECRET #11   107
SECRET #12   111
SECRET #13   117
SECRET #14   125
SECRET #15   135
SECRET #16   145
SECRET #17   159
SECRET #18   167
SECRET #19   173
SECRET #20   177
CHAPTER 4: SERVICES WE PROVIDE   181

Chapter 1

WHO IS A TOP PRODUCER?

There are three constants in life...
Change, choice and principles.

Stephen Covey

Top producing Sales People are easy to pick out from the crowd. They have an underlying confidence and their sales skills come off naturally. In other words they are so good, you don't know you're being sold. They come from all walks of life and really can be all ages. They don't necessarily have big degrees from big colleges and may have never even attended college. They have that aura that makes you want to be near them. They have a constant hunger for the sale and are always preoccupied with ways to obtain the sale. They are hunters who live for the sales kill. They are sought out by their potential employers and valued as a key part of the sales strategy for any company they work for.

It is proven, in any given market or in any given selling environment that 10% of the people does 90% of the business: That 10% are your Top Producers!

Is being a Top Producer something you are born with or are these skills something that can be learned? I say yes to both! There are people who are born with that drive to succeed and there are Top Producers being created every day. It happens for many different reasons. Some may become Top Producers because they landed the right account or were in the right place at the right time. Some may not know they are Top Producers but when in a sales environment realize they were born with the drive and determination necessary to be a Top Producer. Some have known all along they were born to be top of their game!

Now if you are reading this and know that you're not a top producer, we are going to tell you how you can become one. It will be up to you to make it a reality in your everyday life and sustain it.

Now sustaining a Top Producer status is really what makes you a real Top Producer! Some Sales People may be on top for a year or two and then lose their account or their EDGE and presto, you don't see them on the top 10 list anymore. They don't have the skills to sustain the title and it was just luck or circumstance that found them there.

To be a Top Producer you must have that fire and passion deep in your soul, all the time. You plan every day to be and stay successful, it doesn't happen by accident.

To be a Top producer with longevity you have to work at it every day, all day.   A Top Producer with longevity is the "Gold" that every Sales Person strives to mirror and every employer pays dearly to attain and retain. Why? Because having one top producer is like having a selling machine working for you.   A few top producers can be enough at times to run an entire company. And typically, a Top Producer has smooth transactions and happy buyers.

There are definitive skill sets that will get you to the top and keep you there. We are going to teach you those skill sets and we are going to speak directly to New Homes Sales.

Being the best is a daily habit not a hobby.

I send out emails and articles each week. I religiously send them out in order to give value to my clients and perhaps attract new clients. No matter what vacation I may be on or what team I may be training in any given city, I always make a point to send out my weekly emails and do my regular marketing. It's a habit not a hobby. And all good things come with great product, time and consistent effort. Determination and consistency is a huge part of being a Top Producer. Top Producers are willing to change, morph, remap, retool, think outside the box and venture into the unknown to be successful.

We teach New Home Sales Professionals that in tougher markets, they will need to change the way they sell and create new marketing strategies. They will need to work with the clients walking in the door in different ways than they have in the past and cherish those clients with proper and smart follow up and marketing. The days of letting prospects walk in and walk out, leaving your sales to the law of average are long gone.

Can you imagine Sales Professionals who are consistently marketing in their downtime and working the community and surrounding area to attract new buyers? We not only imagine it, we see it happen. We see the transformation through the classes we teach.

We will teach you that if you want to be the best in this business then you will have to change yourself and your habits just as drastically as our markets change. If you keep your mind open to new ideas, the change will not be painful, just different from your current reality. In tougher markets, we have to get back to basics and remind ourselves of why we got into this business to begin with.

Who are you?

Here are some great questions that you need to ask yourself...

- ✓ Why did you get into this business?
- ✓ Do you have the tenacity and know how to stay in this business through all markets?
- ✓ Are you challenging yourself every day?
- ✓ Are you in the top 10% of your company?
- ✓ Do you have a business plan to achieve your success?
- ✓ Are you willing to change what you do every day in order to be successful?

Where are we going?

Over the last 100 years, real estate markets have shown proven and dependable up cycles and down cycles. Here are some estimated time frames based on 100 year history.

- Market Cycles are generally 15 years, 7 or 8 Years in

either direction.
- Approximately two Presidential cycles up and two cycles down for about 100 years

Real Estate cycles have a pattern that is dependable but not always anticipated.

And so the bottom line is if you are going to be in the real estate business, then you should be prepared for real estate cycles.

In order to make it through the cycles of real estate and have a thriving career, you need to be the very best in the business.

1. You need to challenge yourself each day and think of new ways to obtain business.
2. You need to maximize the business already walking in your door.
3. You need to be evaluating constantly your performance and crafting your art. You need to take a look at every step of the sale and make sure you are performing each step thoroughly and efficiently.
4. You need to maximize your entire day, using every minute to be successful.

We'll help you do all of this and more!

Chapter 2

BECOME AN
"EDGE AGENT"

"If you are going to show up,
Then you might as well be first and
You might as well be the best!"

Shirleen Von Hoffmann

ONE QUESTION...

How do you THRIVE in this market or any market?

ONE ANSWER...

Become an "Edge" Agent

Who is an "EDGE Agent"?

At Home Builders AdvantEDGE our certification process creates "EDGE Agents", who are Top Producers. When you have achieved the status of an "Edge Agent", you have reached the pinnacle of your new home sales career. You have reached the position of having all the skills and talent necessary to be a Top Producing New Home Sales Professional. You have reached a position sought out by many Builders and Managers in the industry.

The crest we use to represent Edge Agents includes a Lion, the fiercest, bravest hunter of the forest. If you are an Edge Agent you are a true hunter. You thrive on the hunt for the sale!

An "EDGE" agent is an agent who thinks, acts and sells unlike any other new home sales agent.

"EDGE" Agents are experts in all aspects of new home sales; building rapport, marketing, negotiations, finance, closing and consumer relations. They are equipped with the latest sales techniques.

"EDGE Agents" give the prospects their undivided attention and are very good at building rapport. They realize that having great rapport makes everything associated with the sale easier!

"EDGE Agents" know how to question to build rapport and obtain desires and needs and then sell those needs.

"EDGE Agents" remember facts and details about their prospects and log that data into a system for future marketing.

"EDGE Agents" follow up with prospects in ways that are personal, build value and fill needs, so that they will be remembered above the rest of their competition.

"EDGE Agents" are fearless when it comes to change, innovation, overcoming objections, negotiations and closing the deal!

"EDGE Agents" are never content waiting for the sale to walk through the door… "EDGE Agents" fill their time planning for the sale, getting the sale and closing the sale.   They are true hunters.

"EDGE Agents" are like no other sales agents and ones that Builders will seek out to hire, cherish and retain.

"EDGE Agents" are top producers and make great money in every market whether it is good or bad!

"EDGE Agents" are held in the highest esteem by the Builder and Managers. Everything is easier when you become an "EDGE Agent".

It is our ultimate goal that the changes we teach you, will not only make you more money but will make you a more "in demand" Sales Agent; different from all the rest; the very best in the business; An EDGE Agent!

Ways to become an "EDGE Agent":

It's all very simple and of course you will need to study, apply and pass through the proper courses. But you should get the right frame of mind to begin. Here are a few ways to do that.

Help your customers

Be the leader, the one with the experience and the one with the answers. Be optimistic about real estate as an investment and its recovery. Reaffirm the cyclical nature of real estate but that there is no better investment. Prospects will always remember your positive attitude, experience, leadership and help.

Get closer to your customers

Put yourself in their shoes for a day. Get to understand what they are thinking, their concerns about buying and come up with solutions to their objections.

Position yourself as a resource

Know everything about your homes, your community, financing and your builder. You are an expert on everything and anything that says, "New home". Know more and be more than your competition. Give your prospects that buying experience they are looking for.

Get endorsements from your most loyal customers, and use them in a testimonial

This will authenticate all your claims. Your prospects will be more likely to believe you. Your customers will love you, and will tell others. And your competition will hate you.

Rededicate yourself to the present.

Your ability to win is in direct proportion to your desire to remain a student and the intensity of your attitude and enthusiasm.

This means you need to live in the moment. The market is different now from five years ago and it will be different next month. No matter what the market, dedicate yourself to being in the present and bring your skills to the level you need.

For instance, if you are an Agent in today's market and don't believe you need to know how to use the computer to be in sales, you are dead wrong!

If you find yourself becoming stale or negative, become aware of it immediately and do whatever you need to do to bring yourself to a positive, uplifted position. There is no room for negativity when you are in sales.

Give impeccable service.

Customer Service is one of the most important things you can do to build rapport and get referrals.

- Always do the right thing.
- Always honor your word.
- Always under promise and over deliver.
- Always follow through on what you promise.
- Always go that extra mile, no matter what.
- Always put the client first.

Build relationships for life

For so many years, new home sales agents treated each deal as a single transaction instead of looking at their business as one where they are constantly building long term, sustained relationships.

Let's face it, in our hot market, you didn't have to think of such things because people were waiting in line to buy. You wrote the offer, closed the transaction and moved to the next one without looking back. But now, you need to start looking at all things differently and with a fresh pair of eyes. The order taker sales person is not acceptable and will be gone. You must not only be good, you must be great!

The days of waiting for the buyer to come in, fill the card out, view the models and if they didn't buy just let them go and move on to the next person...are gone, gone, gone! Engaging with each buyer, getting to know their needs and wants, engaging them as you walk through the homes, taking notes, influencing them with your great sales capabilities, pacing the conversation, moving them to locations where you want to tie down the sale, will become the way of life for great sales people.

When a buyer walks in, he needs to have a certain experience and that experience is provided by YOU. It goes back to basics; you want them to remember you over and above all of the other agents in the communities they are visiting that day.

How do you do that?

- ✓ Get out from behind your desk.
- ✓ Walk over to the customers; greet them as if you are pleased to see them.
- ✓ Give them your undivided attention.
- ✓ Find out what motivated them to come to your community.
- ✓ Find out why they are buying and what their needs are.
- ✓ Do they have a home to sell?
- ✓ Get to know them and their families and interests.
- ✓ Create great rapport; make them feel as if you are interested in them and not just in a sale.
- ✓ Don't just forget them and move to the next prospect when they leave. Follow up with them, over and over. They are a precious commodity.
- ✓ Make them remember YOU, the person.

What is it about YOU, your routine, your greeting, and your sales process that makes you different from the next sales person? Let's really think about this question;

How will your prospective buyers remember you and your homes from all the others they may visit that day?

It all starts in the first few critical seconds. You need to sum up your buyers and mirror them, read body language, evaluate eye contact, tonality of voice. If there is more than one person, figure out who is the leader, but don't ignore the other person and come up with your approach to the sale.

It's a lot to do, quickly, but part of your job. How well do you do it? And that's just the beginning of the process. There is so much more.... No worries, we have solutions for you!

CAUTION: To be the best is a combination of all these elements. There is no pill you can swallow that will make the market better, you better, or the customer buy faster. Nor will it make the customer buy from you, rather than the competition. The good news is that you control your destiny. That's why you got into sales in the first place.

We will be starting with the basics and moving through a sale. We do this because we find, through our secret shopping that most Agents are forgetting the basics. You must master the basics in order to be a Top Producer. Top Producers take the basics of a sale and move to a place of perfection. They don't miss steps, therefore steps aren't missed!

We have the answers you need but we need your buy in and commitment in order for you to be a success.

- ✓ We need you to walk along with us, one step at a time and master your skills.
- ✓ We need you to be a sponge and be able to adapt new habits and ideas.
- ✓ We need you to be like a new born baby, learning new things each day with a fresh attitude.

Do all of this and you will reap the benefits this book offers you.

Adapt the Top Producer mentality before you are one. Do the Agent Takeaways we give you, to master your skills. When you master your skills and have the attitude of greatness, you become a Top Producer.

Let's take a close look at the essence of my book and what "Edge Agents" base all of their training on; "Top Producer Secrets".

Let's just start at the beginning of being great, shall we?

Chapter 3

TOP PRODUCER SECRETS

"Being the best is a matter of persistence, insistence,
consistence and fear resistance!"

Shirleen Von Hoffmann

TOP PRODUCER
SECRET #1

GOALS

"Imagine arriving in a foreign country and trying to get to Sales Street without having a road map; You would make a lot of wrong turns or perhaps never get there at all!"

Shirleen Von Hoffmann

Your blueprint for success...
it doesn't happen by accident.

Let's talk about a plan, a blueprint for success.
How many of you have a plan?
How do you get to a location without a map?
What is a map? In essence, it is the written word.
You can't build a home without a blueprint?
How do achieve a dream without a vision?

You have a plan, an agenda, a way to a means, a way to achieve your dream. "EDGE Agents" are top producers and top producers have goals and a plan to achieve those goals.

What are some of the things you need in your Blueprint for success? In a blueprint of a home, you have at least three major components, a floor plan, an elevation and square footage. We are giving you seven goal setting steps as major components in your blueprint for success.

Take some time to write down what your goals are as well as the income you would like to make for the year. What is the difference between a dream and a goal? The written word. Write out a blueprint of the things you will need to do to achieve those goals.

Goal setting is more than simply scribbling down some ideas on a piece of paper. Our goals need to be complete and focused, much like a blueprint. If you follow the 10 goal setting steps, you will be well on your way to building the blueprint to achieve success.

1. Goals should be something you really want

Not just something that sounds good. When setting goals it is very important to remember that your goals must be consistent with your values.

2. A goal can not contradict other goals

For example, you can't buy a $750,000 house if your income goal is only $50,000 per year. This is called non-integrated thinking and will sabotage all of the hard work you put into your goals. Non-integrated thinking can also hamper your everyday thoughts as well. We should continually strive to eliminate contradictory ideas from our thinking.

3. Develop goals in the 6 areas of life

Family and Home	Financial and Career
Spiritual and Ethical	Physical and Health
Social and Cultural	Mental and Educational

Setting goals in each area of life will ensure a more balanced life as you begin to examine and change the fundamentals of everyday living. Setting goals in each area of life also helps in eliminating the non-integrated thinking we talked about in the 2nd step.

4. Write goals in the positive tone

Part of the reason why we write down and examine our goals is to create a set of instructions for our subconscious mind to carry out. Your subconscious mind is a very efficient tool, it cannot determine right from wrong and it does not judge. Its only function is to carry out its instructions. The more positive instructions you give it, the more positive results you will get.

Thinking positively in everyday life will also help in your growth as a human being. Don't limit it to goal setting.

5. Write goals out in complete detail

Instead of writing "A new home," write "A 4,000 square foot contemporary with 4 bedrooms and 3 baths and a view of the mountain on 20 acres of land."

Once again we are giving the subconscious mind a detailed set of instructions to work on. The more information you give it, the more clear the final outcome becomes. The more precise the outcome, the more efficient the subconscious mind can become.

Can you close your eyes and visualize the home described above? Walk around the house. Stand on the porch off the master bedroom and see the fog lifting off the mountain. Look down at the garden full of tomatoes, green beans and cucumbers. And off to the right is the other garden full of mums, carnations and roses. Can you see it? So can your subconscious mind.

6. Make sure your goal is high enough

Shoot for the moon; if you miss you'll still be in the stars. Do make your goals achievable.

7. Write down your goals

Writing down your goals creates the blueprint to your success. Although just the act of writing them down can set the process in motion, it is also extremely important to review your goals frequently. Remember, the more focused you are on your goals; the more likely you are to accomplish them.

8. Create Action Steps

Once you know your goals, you will need to create the action steps necessary to attain those goals. Be very specific about these action steps.

9. Calendar your Action Steps

Put your action steps on your daily calendar to assure that you will fit them in to your day to day routine.

10. Keep yourself open to change

Sometimes we realize we have to revise a goal as circumstances and other goals change. If you need to change a goal do not consider it a failure, consider it a victory as you had the insight to realize something was different.

So your goals are written down. Now what?

Agent Takeaway:

- ✓ Reviewing your goals daily is a crucial part of your success and must become part of your routine. Each morning when you arrive at the office, read your list of action steps and take them from "TO DO" to "DONE".
- ✓ Visualize the completed goal, see the new home, smell the leather seats in your new car, feel the cold hard cash in your hands. Then each night, right before you go to bed, repeat the process. This process will start both your subconscious and conscious mind on working towards the goal. This will also begin to replace any of the negative self-talk you may have and replace it with positive self-talk.
- ✓ Every time you make a decision during the day, ask yourself this question, "Does it take me closer to, or further from my goal." If the answer is "closer to," then you've made the right decision. If the answer is "further from," well, you know what to do.
- ✓ If you follow this process everyday you will be on your way to achieving unlimited success in every aspect of your life.

"Edge Agents" always begin with a successful end in mind, so goal setting and planning is on the top of the list.

TOP PRODUCER SECRET #2

MEET & GREET

"People remember when you make them feel special.
Give them your time,
value and honor them
by using their name.
Name one thing more important,
than that prospect in front of you"

Shirleen Von Hoffmann

Meet & Greet & Creating an Experience

When was the last time you can remember being surprised and delighted by a company and something they did that made you feel special? Our question is this...did they make you a life time client by doing this? This answer is probably 100% YES!

Builders and Sales Agents always need to make the most out of every prospective buyer who walks through the door. They are so valuable. What can you do that is different in your meet and greet, your interactions, your questioning and follow up to make those potentials remember you and come back to buy a home from you? They want an experience and that experience comes from YOU.

We have many ways for you to create an experience for your buyers. Here are just a few.

Take a hard look at your sales models

Buyers' attention to first impressions, senses-nose smells, eyes-visual, temperature-warm, sensory perceptions-feelings and yes...decorating, is so important.

Your Sales Office

How can you make it more welcoming and feel like a comfortable, inviting place for your buyers to sit, relax and chat? Remember to use your senses of sight, sound and smell when you are coming up with your ideas.

Everyone likes being welcomed "Home" into a comfortable environment. Starbucks recently closed for the day and among many changes, they changed the interiors of their stores. In some stores they placed couches where there were tables and chairs before. This one change makes people sit and converse on the couch in the middle of the store and provides a totally different feeling of relaxation, warmth and comfort.

Take a look at your Sales Office. Can you do some rearranging if needed to make it more welcoming? Can you add special touches to make it more welcoming, smell better, look better and be more appealing to your prospects?

Agent Takeaway:

> ➢ Walk into your models and take notice of all of these things as if you were a buyer. Try blindfolding yourself and notice the smell and temperatures. Then take the blindfold off and notice the visual perceptions and the feelings that come over you.

Rethink your meet and greet.

Having a great "Meet and Greet" is the foundation of building rapport with your prospects. Building great rapport is one of the most important things you can do as a Salesperson. Why? Because once you have rapport built with your client, everything becomes easier. The sale, option sales, negotiations, follow up, the construction process, objections and closing all become easier when you build a great rapport.

The "Meet and Greet" is key. So how is your "Meet and Greet?"

At Home Builders AdvantEdge we have been through many communities and you know the one "Meet and Greet" most commonly used?"

"Is this your first time here?"

You should know this one thing...this is not a good "Meet and Greet." It has nothing in it that says we welcome you, thank you for coming, how can I help you?

A great "meet and greet", starts with 3 things;

1. A welcome statement.
2. A name introduction of yourself and one from them with a handshake.
3. An open ended questions using their name at least twice and finding out their needs.

Here is how a great Meet and Greet sounds;

"Hi, Good Morning come on in, Welcome to Emerald Bay, My name is Shelby and yours? (Extend hand for handshake) Julie? Well Julie, welcome to our community we are happy you stopped by today. So Julie tell me, what kind of home are you looking for today? Do you have a size in mind?"

Agent Takeaway:

> ➤ Go visit other subdivisions as a buyer and note how
> you are greeted. What can you do differently to set
> yourself aside? So many say, "What brings you here
> today?" or "How did you find us?" or "Is this your first
> time here"...all of these greetings could be much better.
> How will you be different from the rest?

Implement and practice these sales techniques and they will become a natural, easy part of your sales routine and you will be a Sales Agent builders seek...An "Edge Agent!"

People want to be acknowledged, recognized and remembered. Welcome them to your home by introducing yourself and remembering their names.

Remembering and using names:

The sweetest sound you can use with your prospects is their name.

It is very important to remember to introduce yourself and get their names right away. People love to hear their name being used.

A few things happen when you use and remember names:

> ➤ It makes them feel welcomed.
> ➤ It makes them feel important that you took the time to remember them.
> ➤ It makes them feel as if they are among friends, when you use their name.

How to remember names:

One technique for remembering names is to imprint your brain with the person's name 8 to 10 times within 3 minutes of meeting them.

Listen to "Cathy" say her name.

Look at her, see her face, think; she is Cathy.

Repeat her name by saying, "Cathy, it's nice to meet you."

Begin to use her name. You might say "Cathy, is that Cathy with a 'C' or Kathy with a 'K'?" She could answer, "Cathy with a 'C.'"

Now your brain has been imprinted with the name six times and you have visualized it at least once. Continue to use it on the walk.

Agent Takeaway:

> ➢ Do your best this week to remember the names of all of the prospects you meet.
>
> ➢ Notice the difference in them when you use their names.

TOP PRODUCER
SECRET #3

WALKING THE MODELS

"The statistic is that only 2% of Sales People spend their time walking the models with their prospects; sounds like you might want to take AdvantEDGE of that statistic!"

Shirleen Von Hoffmann

Walking the Models

If you have attended our seminars you know that for every 30 minutes you spend with a prospect your chance of a sale increases by 30%! When are you going to spend this much time with a prospect unless you walk with them?

Touring the models is a wonderful opportunity to spend time with your prospects and you can learn so much about them. This is important for a sale as well as for follow up, so you can market smart! So that is always our first suggestion for Builders and Agents who want to increase their sales.

In a survey of 50 New Home communities in San Diego only 2% of agents walked with the prospects through the models. TWO PERCENT! In this market we found that figure to be very interesting. You know what it tells you? It tells you that your competition is not doing this, so you should be.

Falling in love with your home...

The goal is to sell the buyer and make them fall in love with your home and nothing else at this point. Build a comfortable rapport without interrogating them. Make it feel like a natural process as if you were talking with a new friend. Make sure to listen to all of their dreams and all of their fears and take notes so you can remember them. That is how you can come up with solutions to their problems and become their new best sales person friend with all of the answers and solutions.

Three easy ways to initiate a walk

Some Sales Agents stumble over the very important step of initiating a walk. It is so easy once you know how to do it and you can perform it with ease and confidence.

We all know that as a salesperson when you ask a buyer to do something, it does not always work because it's so easy to say no. But there are a few ways to get people to the models that are easy and will accomplish the goal of doing a model walk.

Here are just a few ways to initiate a walk. Play with these techniques and pick the one that fits your particular personality and style.

THE TEAM LEADER – 95% of the population will follow a leader. After you have asked enough questions to warrant a model walk and to move them to the next step, you can very easily state;

Example: "Let's go together and I will show you a plan I think you will love!" Then you just start walking. Most buyers are expecting that you are going to show them around the models and will follow you as planned.

THE LISTENER - The next way is similar but takes a little more thought on your part. As you ask questions up front, look for clues that match one of your models or floor plans. Get the potential client to talk as much as possible so you know right where you are going to direct them.

Example: Let's say you have a client who says he is looking for a two story but needs the master bedroom to be downstairs. The best way to go about this walk is repeating what he said, "So one of the important things to you in your new home is a two story with a master downstairs, is that correct?" "Great, I'm happy to hear that because we have one I know you will love and they are hard to come by. It's one of our best sellers. Let me show you."

THE INITIATOR – Most people will follow someone who initiates an action because they don't have time to say, "No." An initiator acts quickly and moves with ease and confidence.

Example: After your initial inquiry about the size of the home and number of stories you say, "Well we have two one story models.

Let's go through the first one together and I can tell you about what's included."

Grab a registration card and say, "I'll fill this out for you as we go through the model." Then you just move.

All of these examples get you to the same place which is a Model Walk. The question is, which one works better for you? The bottom line is this; get your buyers into a model or two; practice and hone your skills; keep trying and just do it! Before you know it, you will be a pro.

Questions to ask along the way

You did your probing in the sales office and now you are off to the model walk. As you are walking, there is some precious time that goes by where you can continue to find out more things about your customers. You have a limited amount of time to find out all kinds of information that will either help you make a sale or help you market to a future sale. Make sure to write down all your information so that you remember all the details about your buyers for future marketing. You think you will remember later, but at busy times, you will not!

Here are a few examples of some easy probing questions to ask your potential customers along the way;

Sample Questions;

- *What are the three most important aspects you are looking for in a home?*
- *What doesn't work for you in the home you have now?*
- *Why are you looking for a new home?*
- *What rooms are most important to you and your family?*
- *Where does your family spend most of its time in your home?*

Pause for a Cause

You all have heard a thousand times, "Sell the sizzle." Well how much of your competition is getting their clients to the models? Better yet if they do get them to the models are they doing anything extra? Let's face it, this is your best way to give yourself an edge over the competition.

As you approach the model, a great opportunity arises. It's called the **Pause for a Cause.** Ok, it sounds strange but you probably won't forget it. In this part of the model walk you want to pause at the edge of the driveway of the model and take a moment to slow the pace down. Take in the outside of the home first. Let the prospect build a little momentum for the model tour and make them notice the features your builder has provided on the outside.

By doing this you will be controlling the pace and you will also be spending more comfortable time with the prospect.

Oh and let's not forget you will be setting yourself apart from your competition because they are not doing model walks.

Find special things about your homes that no one else offers or that are unique to your builder and your community. Script these unique items on a sheet of paper and practice a few for each model so you have them ready in your repertoire.

Pause for a Cause sample question.

"Now what do you think about this model and how the architects took the time to show off all of the features above the entry and outside the windows? Didn't they do a great job? You won't find this kind of detail anywhere but here. Can you believe how well this home looks from the street view? Can you see yourself driving up in this driveway every night?"

Sweet Spots

There are spots outside and inside of your homes. Sweet spots are locations that have the best vantage points. In other words, if the architect were walking the home with you, he would stop you in those sweet spots and say, "Look at the home from here, isn't it amazing?"

Well we want you to pick these spots out inside and outside of your homes and use them as a sales tool to pause and take in the views. It also keeps you in control of the pace of the tour.

Agent Takeaway:

> ➢ Go through each model by yourself and find a spot outside, a spot at the entry and a few spots inside the home that give you the best vantage point.
>
> ➢ As you find these spots, look at the floor and literally see and acknowledge in your brain that this is the "sweet spot", the best vantage point to stop your client for viewing this model. Then as you walk your client through and you are in "sales mode", your brain will stop you at these sweet spots automatically.
>
> ➢ Use the "sweet spots" as places to stop your prospect and talk about the view and take in the room and its architectural benefits.

Strategies on entering and being inside the model.

There are some very important steps once you enter the models. Here are just a few rules of the road when it comes to body positioning and what to talk about once inside your models.

- You may open the door but stand to the side.
- Let the client walk in first.
- Never stand in the middle of the room.
- Point out "real life" benefits and features as well. *i.e.: "Now this is a family room that will hold a real family!" "Isn't the size great?" "Didn't you say you had four children? This would be a great room for your large family."*
- Point out features that are not options, like great lighting, well thought out floor plan and wide halls.
- Go through your models and come up with 5-10 things that are unique to that model that you can use, script and memorize.
- Try to set a vision of ownership whenever you can.

How to set a vision of ownership

A Vision of Ownership is when you help your buyers to visualize living in your home. You use statements and questions that help them "see" themselves living there. Because you probed in your sales office and on the way to the models, you should know enough personal information about them to set some vision of ownership statements.

When you do this, you start the "falling in love" process working in their brains. Even when they leave your community, they will still be thinking about it.

Think about when you might have purchased something big in the past and thought about it over and over in your brain. You usually see yourself with it…whether it be driving a certain car or sitting on certain new furniture. Many people are visual and you need to appeal to everyone and help them to visualize whenever you can.

Example of a "Vision of ownership statement"

"You said you love to relax in a hot tub at the end of the day. Then check out the bath tub in this master bath. It is huge and has a view of the backyard! Can you see yourself relaxing in this beautiful tub at the end of the day?"

Asking trial close questions and setting a site.

Once you feel you have enough positive comments and that this is the model for your prospect don't waste time in trying to move the sale to your available home sites for a site tour. Try to set some urgency around this move. Here is an example of a question you can ask that will accomplish this mission.

Example of trial close;

"So do you feel that this model is the home for you and your family? YES, Great! Then once you have finished looking at it, I will show you some lots we have. There are only a few available."

Let them look alone only if you feel they need to.

Once you have shown them the models that you feel fit their needs, go ahead and let them look on their own if they so desire. If things are going well, ask them if they would like to see the next one. If they agree...stay with them! Why not? They are your most important commodity, nothing else should matter. And don't forget, every 30 minutes with them increases your chance of a sale by 30%. And you know your competition isn't doing it, so they are going to remember you and your community and the special attention you gave them that day.

Don't Oversell

Remember to listen to clues your prospect gives you and don't oversell. Talk up the important benefits of your homes and be there to answer questions, but also know when to be quiet and listen! Don't turn into a "Vanna White" It's not fun for you or for them! **Use this time as an opportunity to build rapport.**

The Site Tour

You should always be ready to do a site tour. It is a good idea to have a Site Tour Kit which includes: *(Hard hats, measuring tapes, a disposable camera, Model and plot plan, notepad, pencil, water and a sold sign.)*

Remember to do these things about the site tour;

- ✓ Walk the site. Have a sweet spot picked out where you have the best vantage point.
- ✓ Talk about the surrounding neighborhood.
- ✓ Paint a vision of ownership just like you would inside.
- ✓ Ask site closing questions now.
- ✓ Have a Sold sign ready to pound in the ground!
- ✓ By knowing these steps to showing a model you will not only make your prospects remember you but you **will** increase your sales. It's easy, it just takes practice!

Agent Takeaway:

> Try to increase your "Model Walks" by 70% this week. Notice the difference in how easily you can build rapport.
> Practice relaxing and asking questions and getting to know your prospect instead of "demonstrating". Set visions of ownership.
> Use the walk techniques we have given you and make room in your pocket book for more money from the increased sales you will get!

TOP PRODUCER SECRET #4

BUILDING RAPPORT

"Strategic advantage lies in the
Leverage of being able
to create friendships."

Shirleen Von Hoffmann

Building Rapport

Rapport is a process of building a sustaining relationship of mutual trust, harmony and understanding. This happens through matching the accessing cues from words, eye movements and body language. Rapport is the ability to be on the same wavelength and to connect mentally and emotionally. It is the ability to join people where they are in order to build a climate of trust and respect. Having rapport does not mean that you have to agree, but that you understand where the other person or is coming from.

Rapport – the Key to Influence

Rapport is the key to influence. It starts with acceptance of the other person's point of view, their state and their style of communication. To influence, you have to be able to appreciate and understand the other person's standpoint. And this works both ways: I cannot influence you without being open to being influenced myself.

Rapport as a Philosophy

Rapport works best when it is a philosophy – a way of dealing with people and a way of doing business at all times. Having rapport as a foundation for the relationship means that when there are issues to discuss, you already have a culture in place that makes it easier to talk them through and thus to prevent issues from developing into complaints, objections or problems.

Rapport – the Key to Building Trust

Rapport is achieved when two people can see the other person's viewpoint, appreciate each other's feelings, and be on the same wavelength. We all have different maps of reality – ways in which we perceive the world – and we can only really trust people who look at the world the way we do. If we feel understood, we give people our trust and open up to them more easily. Taking the other person's perceptual position will help you achieve rapport and build trust.

Creating Rapport

To create rapport, it is important to mirror, match, and pace the person or persons with whom you are communicating. In order to do so, it is important for you to open your sensory channels. You can train yourself to build and refine this skill. Opening your sensory channels, provides you with the ability to see, hear, and sense external changes (minimal cues, both verbal and nonverbal) presented by individuals with whom you are communicating.

Establishing a business relationship with a new prospect is a lot like walking a tight rope. Every single move you make has consequences.

When you execute it flawlessly, you're in a perfect position for your next move. However, any misstep on your part sends you into recovery mode. Sometimes you're able to bounce back, but other times you fall off and you are out. Sounds an awful lot like sales to me! The early stages of the sales process can be filled with difficulties but doesn't have to be.

If you try to proceed in a sale without having rapport with the prospect, the entire process is harder. For instance, if you ask for a registration card before you develop rapport, the odds of your getting one go down to a 30% chance. If you have rapport developed and you ask for a card the odds of your getting a card will be 85%.

Everything is easier when rapport is developed. Think about it. When you have good rapport, everything, including questioning, walking the models, getting a card, making the sale, negotiating, closing and handling problems and even asking for referrals, is easier because you have a relationship. It makes the whole sales cycle easier.

How do you develop rapport?

- Ask good questions. Good open ended questions. Do

49

not ask questions which elicit "yes" or "no" answers. Ask questions that get you information.

- Don't make the prospect feel like you are "selling" them. Be yourself as if you were talking to friends.
- Actively listen to them and respond to their needs.
- Be sincerely interested in their needs.
- You need to practice techniques, scripts and prepare like everything depends on it - because it does.

Your prospect is the ultimate judge of the effectiveness of your rapport building. If you don't advance to the next step, your sales routine needs more fine-tuning. When you advance to that next step, you will know your sales routine is working.

Remember this very important statement;

"If you don't build rapport with that prospect,
you probably won't be building a house for that prospect."

Agent Takeaway:

> ➢ Try building rapport before asking for a registration card and see the difference in how many more cards you can collect.

TOP PRODUCER SECRET #5

PROBING & SMART MARKETING

"Perhaps the very best question
that you can repeat, over and over is,
"Did I do my best to maximize my time
and questions to that prospect?"

Shirleen Von Hoffmann

Probe your Prospects

How do you keep information on the buyers walking in your door? Most New Home Agents who bother to get registration cards make most of their notes on the back of the card. That technique just doesn't work for "EDGE Agents." EDGE Agents are smarter than that and want to capture every detail about every prospect so they can follow up with them and smartly market to them.

Do you have a probe sheet that prompts you to ask probing questions and get information from your buyers? If you don't, you should. You can make this form yourself and fill it with all the things you want to know about your prospects and their motivations, lives, hobbies, careers, you name it!

After the prospects leave and their information is fresh in your memory, make notes on that buyer on your probe sheet and enter those notes into your data base. Using this information to market is like gold. When the probe sheet is done in advance, it allows you to simply check boxes and fill in details easily.

You should have a thorough data base of clients with information that goes way beyond the visitor cards that they fill out to tell you how they found you.

Things to have on your prospect probe sheet:

- ✓ Name
- ✓ Address
- ✓ Phone numbers
- ✓ Emails
- ✓ Why they are looking?
- ✓ Do they have a home to sell?
- ✓ Do they have children?
- ✓ Do they work in the area?
- ✓ Why are they looking in your area?
- ✓ Have they purchased a new home before?

✓ How did they hear about your subdivision?
✓ What are they looking for in a home?
✓ What do they do for a living?
✓ What is important to them in choosing a home?
✓ When do they plan to purchase?
✓ Are they first time homebuyers?
✓ What price range are they seeking?
✓ What is the size of home, lot, they are seeking?
✓ When do they plan on moving?

Personal questions like hobbies, sports, recreation, interests, things they like to do on weekends are also very important in selling your community features, building rapport and relationships. All of these items should be on your probe sheet.

With this information you can properly categorize your potential buyer into your data base as a hot, warm or cold prospect. With this knowledge you will know how to market to each category of buyer and not waste your time and energy marketing to the wrong prospect.

It's always nice to receive something personal from a Salesperson. It says, "I remember you, and you are important to me." If they have a dog, send them vet office locations nearby. If they golf, send them a list of courses…you get the picture! Children are a huge sales factor so find out as much as you can about their children. This is the beauty of the Probe Sheet is it allows you to quickly jot down these important personal facts so you can market smart to them in the future!

Agent Takeaway:

- ➢ Make a prospect probe sheet and include the items we have listed including any others details you would like to add.
- ➢ Photocopy it and have it handy for you to grab when talking with prospects.

TOP PRODUCER SECRET #6

HOW TO ASK GREAT QUESTIONS

"You ask questions to
build rapport and gain knowledge;
you build rapport to gain trust;
you gain trust because
together can equal 65% of a sale."
Those are great odds!

Shirleen Von Hoffmann

How to ask great questions

Questions are at the heart of a sale. Ask the wrong questions and you will get the wrong answers. Good open ended questions uncover facts and motives for buying.

The Salesperson who develops rapport and creates friendships by asking questions, gets the sale because people love to do business with friends.

How do you know that you have mastered asking great questions? When the prospect says, "That's a great question. No one has asked me that before!" If you hear that, you are on the right track to being a master.

Do you remember some of your basic sales training when it comes to the types of questions to ask? As you recall, there are two basic types of questions. They are closed ended questions and open ended questions or what I call "disclose" questions.

To close or disclose...that is the question!

The individual situation and type of information you are trying to get often dictates which type of question to use. There are times when you want to ask closed questions to lead a conversation to a place you want it to go or to get a quick answer. However, during the initial relationship process, open ended questions should dominate.

Closed Questions

Closed ended are restrictive questions that can be answered very quickly with a simple yes or no or a very limited response. This type of question is useful for obtaining a specific bit of information, data or validation. They are often used in the closing process as well. Examples include questions like:

Do you want me to order our backyard landscaping package for your new home?

Do you prefer our next appointment to be on Monday or Thursday?

Open Ended Questions (Disclose Questions)

Open-ended questions do not lead the customer and they do not require a simple answer. Open ended questions seek to gain a better understanding of the customer by getting them to reveal much more about their objectives, needs, current situation and personality profile. Examples include questions like:

Can you tell me the top six things you are looking for in your new home?

Tell me about the things do you not like about your current home.

What are the important hobbies, sports and holidays that you do in your home?

There is a real talent to asking questions without making people feel they are being interrogated. That's why practice, preparation and scripting is very important. When you master and practice the questions, then the delivery should just roll off your tongue as if you were talking to friends.

Putting your Questions together

When you put your fact finding questions together, make sure they include things that concern your buyer.

Here are some topics you can use:

○ Peace of mind
○ Dissatisfaction

- o Desired outcome
- o Children
- o Careers
- o Commuting
- o Quality
- o Price
- o Location
- o Passion
- o Motives
- o Desires
- o Fears
- o Family
- o Community

It's easy when you have topics in mind. Then you can lay your questions out like this:

- o What do you look for...?
- o What have you found...?
- o What makes you choose...?
- o What has been your experience...?
- o What is the one thing you would improve...?
- o What are the deciding factors when...?
- o What would you change about...?
- o Tell me about...?
- o How do you feel about?
- o What would your top 5 needs list be?

These are simple rules about a simple concept and yet it is amazing how many sales people, even experienced sales people forget to apply them. Sales are not easy especially when the economy is struggling.

Practice asking great open ended questions for 30 days and you will begin to see the real rewards; Sales.

Agent Takeaway:

> ➢ Print these ten simple sample open ended questions. Fill in your subjects and practice them in your downtime until the questions are natural and easy for you to use with your prospects.

Questioning to Qualify

Questioning to qualify is essential in a sale and can be used for multiple purposes. Before you invest too much time, you need to find out if you have a qualified buyer. Once you have buying signals and before you write a contract you should qualify the prospect. You must know your financing options and have prequalification skills. When you put them together with the right questions you have a winning combination.

Qualifying question types

You will need to have qualifying questions for credit, down payment, income and debt. Having these questions in a particular order that flows from one to the next is important as well.

You want to know you have a good prospect to validate moving forward with the sale and be able do it quickly so you can get back to the fun of the sale!

Credit questions

Try this for a great credit question, "Tell me about your credit, do you know your credit score?" Then listen and pay attention. The answer you hear is important. If they stutter and stammer, "Well I had some issues in 2005", you probably have credit issues and need the prequalification of your lender. If they say with confidence, "Oh, I have a 700 fico score", most likely they do. Body language is everything in this line of questioning.

Prequalifying Questions

A great qualifying opener question is, "Thinking about your budget, what payment do you think you can afford?" This question really will tell you if your prospect is informed, realistic, prepared and more. You will be able to tell by the answer. This question also will open the door to other qualifying down payment questions, like this," How much money do you have for your initial investment in this home?" When you get that answer it will lead you to gross income and debt qualifying questions.

Let your Lender take it from here

Once you have your qualifying questions and put them in order, you should be able to prequalify a prospect in a few minutes and move back to the sale. Let your Lender handle the details of financing. As soon as you know you have a deal, move on.

Qualifying can be used as a Close

Sometimes the "Have you been to a lender to be prequalified?" question challenges the prospect and works well as a diversion with those who are giving you objections to the sale. This technique is often used as a backbone with many good Sales Representatives and many companies to create a diversion and urgency.

Knowledge is power

Here is something else to remember about qualifying and questions. The more knowledgeable and confident you are as an Agent, the more solutions you can provide to the prospect. The more solutions you provide, the more the prospect will have confidence in you over other Agents who don't have that same knowledge.

Agent Takeaway:

> ➢ We want you to come up with your own set of qualifying questions; one for credit, one for payment, one for income and one for down payment.

Closing Questions

Thousands of books have been written on closing. The long and short of it is; if you don't know how to close, you had better rethink your career choice.

A definition of a closing question is; Asking a question which confirms the sale.

Here is the key. After you ask the closing question, be quiet and listen! Whoever speaks first, loses.

Buying Signals

As soon as you get questions from the buyer regarding timelines, scarcity, incentives, financing, you have buying signals.

As soon as you see buying signals you have the green light to try some trial closes to check the pulse of the sale.

How to construct a closing question

The idea is to try and construct your questions so you don't get a "NO". What you want is either a "YES" or more information from your prospect so you can further question & develop rapport if needed.

Formulate your questions in a way that address the prospect's main desires.

Example of a closed question: We have the model you like only available on a few different lots. Would you like to go to the location of these lots?

Example of an open question: We have the model you like on a few different lots. What are some of the preferences you have in mind for your lot location?

In Sales "NO" is the enemy

You can see that if you use the first example it is very likely you may get a NO. When you use the second example you will get more information about that buyer's preferences.

Trial Closes

Don't ever be afraid to use Trial closes to work your way to closing questions. Trial close questions should be indirect using skills like setting visions of ownership and small questions asked throughout the presentation.

An example of a Trial close using this technique would be;

*"Can you visualize your family celebrating a
birthday around this dining room?"*

Agent Takeaway:

> ➢ We would like you to come up with three trial close
> questions you feel comfortable using on an everyday
> basis.

TOP PRODUCER SECRET #7

FOLLOW UP

"Think of follow up as an opportunity to do something your competition isn't doing.
I can guarantee you, you will be right!"

Shirleen Von Hoffmann

Follow Up

Most Sales Agents don't look forward to follow up but if you want to close the sale, it's usually necessary. Think of follow up as something you can do to get more sales and make more money. That should make it an easier task.

The more organized you are in advance with your marketing material, the easier it is to follow up. Few potential customers will decide right away and before spending a lot of money to buy a home. Prudent people prefer to think the matter over or look around quite a bit.

Your job is to get prospects who have left your community to come back again and that's where follow up comes in.

If you don't follow up, you will probably become a blur in their memory like the rest of your competition. And if you become a blur, then you have just wasted your time and money and the Builder's time and money. Don't forget if you can't remember that prospect then they probably don't remember you either!

Think Self Employed

New home sales agents need to think of themselves as self employed like a resale agent. A resale agent comes up with a plan for obtaining buyers and executes that plan EVERYDAY.

It all starts with YOU

You are the key to marketing. You are the one and only contact with the prospect. When you market to your prospects you set yourself apart from your competition. It is proven that the Salesperson who markets and follows through is the Salesperson who gets the sale!

Knowing that it is very expensive in time, effort and money to walk one prospect in the door and knowing the Agent who follows up is the one who's likely to get the sale, you should never let a prospect walk out of the door without having all of their contact information in hand so you can follow up with them.

Always get a registration card; here's how;

Don't ask for the card upfront; ask later in the sales process, when you have earned the right to ask for their information. When you ask too soon, before you have built rapport, people are hesitant and chances are 80% will say, "NO." Once you get a "NO" you seldom get a second chance. It's much better to change your routine to ask at the middle or end of the model walk once you are back in your office and doing trial closing. Your odds of getting a card go up to 75% "YES."

Another approach is; don't ask, just slide the card over and nicely say "(Use Name), Please fill this out for me and tell me how you found us, it's important for us to know you and how you found us. In the meantime I will grab you some water!" Have a smile on your face the whole time. Again, if rapport is built this scenario will be easier.

Distinguishing Hot from Cold Leads

Before you decide to follow-up on any new contact, you should have some way to determine which ones even merit the effort. For example, some people will waste your time and never buy. They may not know what they want, or they may be trying to cleverly get free ideas from you. Others simply don't know how to give a direct "NO!" Remember that every moment wasted on a dead end can be used to find a promising new contact.

A cold prospect doesn't ask for details, doesn't give eye contact, doesn't show interest or give you buying cues and they are non committal throughout the presentation. They may be just looking at decorating or spending an afternoon getting remodeling ideas. In any case you should still follow up with a "Thank You" and a buyer referral program flyer.

A warm prospect may be someone who has a house to sell but really wants to buy a new home. You can help them with follow up on tips to sell their home and they will appreciate that kind of follow up. You can also refer a Realtor to them for some advice on listing. You don't want to lose contact with these prospects and they can be your insurance for sales in the future. Send them 5-10 marketing pieces in a six month period and a phone call every two-three weeks just to check in.

A hot prospect may be someone who is ready to buy, a first time homebuyer possibly. You want to really focus your follow up marketing on these prospects. They should get a minimum of 10-20 marketing pieces and one phone call a week from you in a in a six month period. Once a week contact is essential and marketing can be gauged if you are getting them back in the door or hearing from them.

All prospects should get a "Thank You" and a buyer referral program flyer

Types of Follow Up

Usually the best follow up tool, right off the bat is a "Thank You" phone call. After that a personalized letter, "Thanks for visiting" or some other follow up is great! Email and faxes are great too but can be easy to ignore or be missed by the prospect.

Phone calls are quick, convenient and allow you to get instant feedback from your prospect. If you don't reach your prospect, find a time that you can call back rather than leaving a message. Try to set goals for each conversation before you make the call and leave some reason to follow up again with the prospect.

If you want your prospect to remember you and your community, you might look for creative ways to keep in touch. Having learned much about your prospect during your initial meeting, you can pass on information about their sports, activities, children, pets, community interests. The more personal you make the follow up, the more your client will appreciate it and the more you will start to build rapport.

Here are twenty topics ideas you can use to follow up;

- Great financing details
- Builder Specials
- Sporting facilities
- Children's sports and interests
- Schooling
- Golfing, baseball and football facilities
- Walking & Hiking Trails
- Shopping Centers
- Local lakes, parks & recreation
- Local Business, restaurants
- Upcoming Community Events
- Past buyer comments on living in your community.
- Flyer with Tips for listing & selling your home.
- Flyer with Tax advantages of homeownership
- Local Veterinarians
- Local Hospitals & Doctors
- Lists of employers in your community
- Builder list of communities
- Builder Resume and list of accomplishments
- A letter asking for the sale

Finally, keep careful notes pertaining to each of your calls, follow ups and any details that will help you keep track of your work. You never want to send the same thing twice. You will need to create a system that works for you.

Talking about potential systems...make sure you not only have a mail program but an email campaign program. Ask your prospects which way they preferred to be contacted and follow up with them that way. Some might want you to text them, so you should make sure you have texting capabilities on your phone.

The world is emailing now and you should be marketing both ways via mail and email. Your email flyers are free of postage costs and there are numerous contact management companies who will help with high end flyers and send them out for you on certain specified dates. Google them and get a feel for how they work.

When doing three types of follow up; email, mail and phone, you are assured of getting more sales than your competition and the Client will be sure to remember YOU over the competition.

There are tons of marketing/data based programs you can buy that will make the process easier and we provide a full day seminar just on that topic in our EDGE Agent accreditation program. You can purchase a system or come up with your own. The idea is to get a program and start working it immediately.

It takes time and energy but it will be the most important thing you do, that sets you apart from your competition. The goal with data basing your clients is to get them to walk in again and make them buyers. Utilize the advertising dollars your builder is spending to attract buyers.

Follow Up for a close

There's no point in following up unless you are pressing to close the sale each time you make contact. "Touching base" is not enough and is for sales amateurs. You however are a top producer and know that you need to move the prospect closer to the sale each time you follow up in order to get the sale!

You had better believe that other sales agents are not doing prospect follow up as a part of their daily routine. Just by doing this one thing, it will make a huge difference in your sales and marketing and bring you more buyers than those who have no contact. You will be a better sales person and you will be making a difference in a tough market. Builders will notice your efforts and YOU will be one of the 10% left and working each day towards your success and your goals.

Agent Takeaway:

> ➤ Make it a goal and promise to yourself to start following up on every prospect, right now.
> ➤ Build a database and a marketing system through flyers ideas we have given you...and start using it right away.

TOP PRODUCER SECRET #8

MOVING FENCE SITTERS

"When you create value
you create urgency.
One goes hand in hand with the other.
Sell your value and
you have sold urgency.
Give away your value and
you give away your urgency.
Got it?"

Shirleen Von Hoffmann

Creating Value

The single biggest obstacle you will encounter in a tough market is "fence sitters." These are people sitting on the side lines waiting for the best market to get the best deal. It can be a real foe for the Salesperson who has never been through a tough market and not learned the skills to push these buyers off the fence.

There are two steps to moving fence sitters, creating Value and Creating Urgency.

The best kind of value you can create is creating an experience, creating visions of ownership, taking them on model walks and especially site tours. Once you start them dreaming of owning your home, the falling in love process begins. It is incomparable to anything else and will make your job much easier.

Of course, once someone falls in love with your home, that value is established and your job should be easy. But it is not always so easy so you must know how to create value.

When you are talking about value remember, "what is valuable to me, might not be valuable to you." So you must know lots of ways to create value. Here are some other ways to create value;

Your community

Why do your buyers love living there? Have Buyer testimonials.

Schools, shopping, amenities

Schools are a big hot button for people with families. Shopping and amenities are also huge selling points for everyone.

Employers and commuting

Some people will buy because their employer is nearby or they may want to work for an employer nearby. It is also a great resale tool to have large employers in your community.

Green Options in your homes

This is a hot topic right now. If you have not studied up on all of the green items your builder puts in his homes, ask your sales manager to have a special meeting on it so vendors can point out those items and why they are important.

Energy Efficient items in your homes

This is another hot topic, right now. People want to save every dime they can by having energy efficient appliances and homes. If you know your facts this really could be the tipping point that sells your home.

Your Builder

Number of years in the business, number of communities and awards all make a big difference in creating value.

Your quality product

Warranties, customer service awards, options included or not, major features the builder uses.

Your reputation

Customer testimonials, community and builder reputation and community footprints all matter when it comes to your reputation.

Price

People love getting a good deal. Be ready to tell them how and why they are getting such a great buy on your home.

Your competition

Check out your surrounding competition and be ready and able to quote what your differences are and why you are better, not bashing them, just stating facts. Like this, "As you tour our models you will notice our floor plans are unique and create great living space. You won't find that with our competition." That will set seeds for your buyers to watch for your superior features.

Creating Urgency

Before moving on to creating urgency, ask yourself,

"Have I created enough value for my prospect to move to the next step?"

The second step to moving fence sitters is Creating Urgency.

When trying to move fence sitters always remember people want what others have and what they can't have. Fear of loss and anticipation of gain, thus the reason to create urgency.

We have to create urgency in a non urgent market because without it, there's no movement. In other words, prospects have to believe that their needs and wants are going to be met and that there's some compelling reason to do it now.

Think about when you have bought something you desire, what are your motivations for buying? Usually it starts with desire and ends with affordability. Then move to getting what you want, at a good deal, at the right time. You've got to come up with a plan that will be compelling enough to move people, get their attention, connect to them, their visions, and their values and move them off the fence.

Creating urgency in a non urgent market is a challenge but by no means impossible. Creating urgency starts from the moment your buyer walks through the door.

Attitude

You and your product must look ready to go; you must be "on" and look fresh. You must have your attitude in a place that creates urgency even when you haven't had a sale in a month! Never portray "it's a slow market" to a prospect. Never portray you or the builder is desperate to make a deal. That is not sales, that is giving away all your strategy and power. When asked about the market, here's a great response, "Well as a matter of fact our community is selling very well, due to the tax credits, interest rates and pricing advantages. People are realizing now is the time to buy! We hardly have any inventory left to sell at this point."

Your community and buyer experience

Make sure your community, models and office look polished and ready to do business. You should always look and be busy but always making time for your prospect. Pay attention to all the senses your buyers experience in your models, sight, sound, smell, taste and touch. Remember to "create an experience" from our previous training. When you create an experience buyers will remember your community over and above all the rest. Build an experience, and then build value, motivation and urgency.

Here are some other ways to create urgency;

Scarcity - "Not much standing inventory"

Limited product - "Only one of that model available"

Limited time - "Builder will only honor this special on sales closing in 30 days."

Limited availability- "Nothing available now but will have a release next week. Let me put you on my list."

Show your prospect that this is the time to buy. This is how;

Interest rates are at their lowest levels since?

Prices are at their lowest since?

Tax Advantages of buying save you ? dollars per month versus renting.

Tax Credits for buying allow you enough to decorate your home with new furniture!

Incentives by the seller will allow you to pay for options or closing costs that will save you thousands of dollars.

Now, if you have trust and you've removed doubt and you've created urgency, we need to continue to build desire or the "falling in love" process. Get out, get them on a site tour and do some visions of ownership.

Agent Takeaway:

> ➤ Take a look at the nine examples we have listed and think about your community.
> ➤ We want you apply these urgency items to your community and be ready to utilize them to create urgency when you need to.

TOP PRODUCER SECRET #9

MOVING CONTINGENCIES

"Contingencies will always be
a part of your life;
so you might as well do what you can
to make them a short part of your life!"

Shirleen Von Hoffmann

Resale Agent Artillery

You need to have about four resale Agents that you work with, that you can recommend for listing your buyers' properties. By working with at least four, you can have good choices to pick from. If you refer an Agent, they are an extension of you and your reputation so be careful who you choose to work with. Interview potential Agents and make your expectations of them very clear.

Their Services

When you interview Agents they should be able to give you a list of their services and what they do when they receive a listing from you. Larger firms may have a larger breadth of buyers they can reach in different cities. It is important that they work with you and the seller to optimize ideas to move the home quickly. You will all be one big team.

Here are a few things that you should have as requirements of service to work with you:

Communication

You must have clear and frequent communication from them and with your buyer. They should copy you on all communication with the seller.

Seller Preparation

Psychologically, the Selling Agent needs to prepare the seller to be a seller and has to prepare a plan for selling the house. All parties must understand the home, the market and where the competition is.

They should have a marketing and advertising strategy and a pricing decrease/incentive strategy. Upfront two things should be clear; what the plan is and what the seller is willing to do to sell the home.

Price properly

Make sure they have researched the surrounding market place. Plan this step with the Agent. The listed price should be in bottom third of its market in order to sell.

Advertising requirements:

Internal Realtor site
All Local Newspapers
Internet sites: Craig's List, Realtor.com, Yahoo.com
Metrolist-MLS.com
Any and all local real estate magazines.

Follow up surveys to agents

You should send each agent who shows the property a follow up survey and one dollar cash or lottery ticket to complete the survey. If a constant message comes through from the agents, (i.e. price is too high, home smells bad...) make the necessary fixes to the home.

Flyers to MLS meetings weekly

Make sure they get flyers distributed each week at multiple listing service (MLS) meetings without fail.

Open Houses

Buyer open houses can help in a really slow market. A better idea is to have Realtor open houses. Realtors go on tours weekly. They can do a flyer regarding the Realtor open house and offer brunch items or lunch items...agents love food and drink.

Agent Takeaway:

> ➤ We want you to work on finding your four resale agents to work with.
> ➤ Prepare your own list of service requirements you will need and have them come in to discuss working together.

Moving the Contingency

You should have a flyer, full of tips to help your buyers with homes to sell. It should include things like this;

Staging

Staging is critical in this market. If the home is vacant, the home will look bare. Add some pieces of furniture and plants. Make sure you have a place for the buyers to sit down, relax and discuss buying the home.

Clean out the Clutter

If the home is occupied, clean out the clutter and rearrange heavy furniture. Think of it as having to compete with area homebuilder models.

Smells, Spots and Decorating

Make sure the home is clean and smells good. Get rid of spots on carpeting and make sure carpet has been cleaned recently. New dish and bathroom towels, new bed comforters and fresh paint are small investments that can go a long way.

Front Door and Entry

Make sure the front door is clean, painted and the key works easily. A nice smell should greet upon entry. First impressions are everything.

Lower the price

Each week, lower the price in small increments. On many of the automatic search pages this will create an email to buyers as a new listing. Better to drop $100 each week rather than $10,000 after 10 weeks.

Pay higher commissions

Offer to the buyer's agent a full 3% or more commission. Doubling the commission to ANY agent that brings an acceptable offer that closes in 30 days can work well in a tough market when agents are hungry.

Offer buyer incentives

By offering incentives like 2-1 buydowns, you can help qualify more buyers for your home by lowering the qualifying rate. By offering to pay closings costs, you help those buyers who might not have enough money to close, therefore opening the window of opportunity to more buyers It's all about opening windows of opportunity to as many buyers as possible.

Making the incentives easy to understand

Phrasing the buyer incentive in different ways can also be more appealing. For instance;

- "$10,000.00 cash back to decorate your new home!"
- "Seller to make buyer payments for six months!"
- "Seller to pay for buyer closings costs and a portion of down payments!"

All of these examples make the incentive easier to understand.

Always make sure home is fully accessible

If you make it too hard for people to see your home, they might pass the opportunity and see someone else's. Remove your valuables, have your agent put on a lock box and let them know they can view at any time.

Color Picture Flyers and more...

Have high quality color flyers created. You want to attract buyers from the street to the inside of your home. Name your home and have it on the heading of the flyer. It just may help the buyer remember your home over your neighbor's. Not putting a price on the flyer will encourage the prospect to call the agent for a price, which is what you want. Keep the flyer box full at all times. Utilize both sides of the flyer. (ie: financing payment options could be displayed on reverse of flyer.)

Agent Takeaway:

> ➢ We want you to come up with your own flyer, with these tips and more to help your buyers who have homes to sell with listing their homes.

TOP PRODUCER
SECRET #10

MARKETING YOU AND
YOUR BUILDER

"A huge part of any sales job is creating and executing a
marketing and advertising plan.
What makes New Home Sales People different? Here's one
thing; the Builder is spending a lot of time and money
to help you out!"

Shirleen Von Hoffmann

Marketing You and Your Builder

Sell your product and all of its benefits and features, sell yourself and sell your builder, your builder's reputation and years of experience. Talk about all of your great buyers who live there and the great community you are in, schools, shopping, parks, and any positive details the builder is providing to new buyers. Those are the most important things you should be talking about at this point.

Who are the prospects walking in your Door?

Do you know who your buyer is? Is there a buyer pattern? Do you get to know prospects that come in? Do you know where they come from and log it on a map? Do you keep a data base so you can market prospects? Do you have a contact management program you use to keep track of who you are marketing to, what you send and when you sent it? Are you sending prospects marketing material in your down time? Studies prove you should be contacting prospects who have come through your models at least 10 times for them to remember you.

Zero in on a Marketing Source

When you keep track of who and where your prospects come from you can discover loads of information. If you find a particular common source of prospects coming through your door, make sure you develop a marketing plan for that source. For instance, if you have a lot of prospects coming from a certain neighborhood or a certain location you can create a marketing plan for that source.

Value of a Prospect

The goal of follow up with prospects that walk through your door and walk out, is to get them to walk in again and make them buyers. Your Builder has spent huge amounts of money in advertising to attract prospects to walk in the door. These prospects are the easy part of your job because they come right to you with no effort. You simply must sell, market and follow up with these prospects when they leave your community.

Prospect Follow Up

The value in a data base is the quality of the information. That means information entered must be valid and then as the relationship develops and you find out further data about your buyers you must keep up the database. You should have a tickler or contact management system that tells you what you have to mail out each day and what you have mailed out in the past and to whom.

Probe Sheets

As we have said before, a Probe Sheet is a form that has all of your buyer information pre-printed so you just check the boxes that apply to your prospect. Probe sheets should have name, address, ages, phone numbers, interests, home requirements, number and ages of children, hobbies, sports, employers, birthdays, emails... Putting notes on the back of a registration card is not acceptable; you need to be better than that.

You may not get all the information that is listed on a probe sheet all at once but keep it close by and add to it as you discover more about your prospect. Take along your probe sheet on a model walk and have one handy after you have met with a buyer to record all the information you just learned.

For example; If you hear your buyers has children interested in soccer, that should go on the probe sheet so you can follow up with a list of local soccer fields at a later date.

Follow Up and Marketing Programs

> ➢ You must have a mail campaign
> ➢ An email campaign
> ➢ A social networking campaign

> ➤ A phone campaign
> ➤ And an outside marketing campaign

Utilizing social networks like Facebook, Linkedin, Twitter can get the word out about your community. You can create web pages on these sites pretty easily. You can use the page to represent your community and talk about specials or any events you have going on. Invite your happy buyers to become fans of the pages you create.

Marketing your Builder

Make sure you have marketing material that you can use to market your builder. Your builder has years of performance, a resume and is involved in charitable organizations and the community. Make sure you touch on all of these facts as it is important to potential buyers. Use this marketing material as one of the follow up items to prospects.

Agent Take Away:

> ➤ We want you to set up a follow up system to make sure you are following up with your prospects.
> ➤ We want you to get cards and follow up with a Thank You for everyone who visited. On the Thank You we want you to share a personal note to let the prospect know you remembered them.

Marketing to your Community
How can you market in your community to get business?

An easy source for marketing is the buyers living in your community; the people who have bought from you and their family and friends. Most people like to live near their family and friends, so ask for referrals! Here's an easy idea;

1. First make sure you have all the emails of your buyers in a database.
2. Email them on a regular basis with Email articles of interest, links or other cool stuff of value, (not spam), articles they will appreciate like budgeting, home maintenance, community information...use your imagination. This establishes you as an expert and makes them think of you when they think of Real Estate.
3. Have a few different flyers prepared on your referral program and send two articles of interest vs. one referral program flyer.
4. Plan a monthly event for them to bring in their friends and family and give them something for coming. This doesn't have to be expensive. Example; Come by this weekend and bring your friends and family. You can enter a raffle for a free gift certificate valued at $_____ to all of our buyers who bring in family and friends this weekend!

You can also market to small businesses in your community. Here some ideas;

1. Become involved in your community, organizations and all functions happening in your community. Attend events and come with three great questions ready to go. Be sure they begin with, "What's the one thing?" "What's your favorite?" and "What was the best part about?"
2. No matter where you go – the mall, church, out to dinner, the gym - always have your business cards and some brochures with you.

3. Be able to give an unforgettable personal introduction of yourself and commercial for your community in 10 seconds, 30 seconds and 60 seconds.
4. Invite owners and employees of small businesses to your events and ask them if you can put flyers up advertising these events in their business.
5. Make sure your business cards and flyers are everywhere, on every bulletin board wherever you can place them for free.
6. If you are buying gift certificates for events buy them from popular businesses in your area and let the owner know you are doing this. Business is a two way street and they may let you advertise your events more easily.
7. Talk to everybody. Don't sell them; don't probe them, just make friends. Make friends with everybody. Because people buy from people they like first. Make yourself known as the real estate expert in this community.
8. Do volunteer positions with organizations
9. that are relevant to getting business. Be a visible leader to whom others can come to for help.

Agent Take Away:

> ➢ We would like you to start putting your database of past buyers together so you can start marketing to them.
> ➢ We also want you to market yourself and your community to five different businesses in your community.

Marketing to Past Communities

Marketing to your builder's past communities is a warm lead because they are already familiar with your company

In most cases, your Builder has built many other communities in the past.

When you start marketing to these communities, it is like a warm lead because the people living there are familiar with your Builder, your product and your customer service.

In order to start marketing to your Builder's past communities you should:

1. Be able to pinpoint a community or communities that fit your buyer profile, get the street coordinates so you can provide them to your title company.
2. Have a resume of the Builder, prepared by your Marketing Department, showing all accomplishments, awards, years in the business, projects being built and charitable causes he is involved in.
3. Work with your Title company to get a list via CD and mailing labels of names and addresses of all the homeowners in the communities you have pinpointed to be your marketing targets.
4. Have two special offers that you have prearranged with the Builder to offer to these clients. The first special should reward them for buying from you again and the second special should reward them for referring you to a family or friend that purchases a home from you. All builders usually have a referral program in place that will suffice. Just note, in tough markets these rewards have become priced aggressively.
5. Have a flyer prepared by your Marketing Department that appeals directly to these buyers and tells them you are aware they are a customer and appreciate their patronage

and want to reward them for being so. You should include your repurchase special and your referral special in this flyer.

6. Have a great cover letter talking up your Builder and your Community and the reasons why people love living there and why they should buy there. You can get creative with this and use your sales skills to appeal to their current insecurities.

   For example; If you are targeting an older community you can say something like, "Out with the old and in with the new!" or appeal to them with your newer energy savings and efficiencies.

This campaign should be relatively easy to put together working with your Builder, Marketing Department and Title Company and one new sale will make it worth your time and effort.

Keep in mind, past clients are the easiest to sell again and again as long as they were happy with their experience the first time._

Agent Take Away:

> ➤ We want you to pinpoint a past community to market to.
> ➤ Contact your title company and get mailing labels & the database for this community.
> ➤ Come up with a flyer, referral program and cover letter. So you can start mailings in your down time.

Marketing to focused Employers:

Local employers and older neighborhoods are like gold to you!

Many times you have some substantial employers in the area where your community is located. Many people like the idea of no commute, especially these days. You can meet with human resources of these companies and ask if you can come in the lunch room during lunch times and market your community. You really want to use your sales skills to win over Managers to get inside; it will be well worth it in the long run. Think of innovative ways to get an appointment with them and meet face to face.

You should be prepared to offer a special bonus to their employees.

Sometimes it is a good idea to take your lender along to perform "free" pre-qualifications.

You can also ask if you can offer your special bonus to their employees and include it in their paystub envelopes and/or if you can leave flyers in the lunch room or on the bulletin board.

Marketing to focused Neighborhoods

You can look outside your community into older neighborhoods that are 7-15 years old. Your goal is to attract people who are ready to move up or tired of their old home and want a new home or need a lifestyle change.

Once you locate a community that you feel fits your community move up profile, you can work with your marketing department to come up with a great flyer that will appeal to your targeted market.

With that done you can give the street coordinates to your title company and they can pull a farm list for you. The title company can actually print you mailing labels or provide you with a CD of names and addresses of this community. You should get both so you can download the names in your contact program for future marketing and use the labels to mail your first marketing piece.

As an example, *if you have a gated community with an HOA that takes care of lawns search out a community to market to that has many seniors who might appreciate those amenities.*

Agent Takeaway:

> ➢ We want you to choose and work on getting on the "inside" of one employer in your surrounding community.
> ➢ We also want you to find one existing neighborhood you want to market focus on.

TOP PRODUCER
SECRET #11

ACTIVE LISTENING

"When you really listen, you find out needs and wants.
Remember, people aren't interested in what you have to sell,
they are interested in what they need and want.
Sell them what they need and want!"

Shirleen Von Hoffmann

Active Listening

Active listening is a way of listening and responding to another person that improves mutual understanding. Often when people talk to each other, they don't listen attentively. They are often distracted, half listening, half thinking about something else.

Active listening is a structured form of listening and responding that focuses the attention on the speaker. The listener must take care to attend to the speaker fully, and then repeat, in the listener's own words, what he or she thinks the speaker has said. The listener does not have to agree with the speaker, he or she must simply state what they think the speaker said.

Active Listening should be going all of the time in a Real Estate purchase. So many sales people make the mistake of talking and not listening. Active listening is one of the most important sales skills you should have in your artillery. People speak at 100 to 175 words per minute but they can listen intelligently at 600 to 800 words per minute, this is why listening can be so difficult; the mind races faster than people can speak. The solution is to listen with a purpose. You listen with a purpose in order to gain information, obtain directions, understand the needs of others, solve their problems, share their interests, support them, sell them and close them. All of these elements are important in creating a trust relationship with your buyer.

Active listening has several benefits. First, it forces people to listen attentively to others. Second, it avoids misunderstandings, as people have to confirm that they do really understand what another person has said. Third, it tends to open people up, to get them to say more. If they feel you are really attuned to their concerns and wants to listen, they are likely to explain in detail what they feel and why. If both parties do this, the chances of being able to develop a solution to their mutual problem becomes much greater.

Active Listening is very hard for Sales People so you must focus and put all other duties and distractions out of your mind and pay attention. Easier said than done, but you can do it!

The HEAR model stands for hear, empathize, analyze and respond, all essential to active listening. Use it to better understand the facts, ideas and feelings of the speaker and to help the speaker clarify their own thoughts, problems and solutions.

H – Hear the speaker's words
Listen attentively to their words and feelings
Keep an open mind. Avoid letting your own feelings, attitudes or opinions interfere with your ability to listen. Do not evaluate, censor or try to monopolize the conversation.
Do not interrupt. It is important to listen to the speaker's entire thought before you respond.

E- Empathize; put yourself in their shoes
Display an interest in their point of view, even or maybe especially if it differs from your own.
Listen for facts, ideas, and feelings.
Listen for the thoughts behind the words.
Check for understanding, by paraphrasing the facts as well as the speaker's position. ("Are you saying that we need to improve our data base practices based on the records you looked at and the conversations you've had with staff across the organization?")

A – Analyze the speaker's words and thoughts.
Listen for the thoughts behind the words. Thinking is faster than speech. Use your extra "thought time" to summarize, review and anticipate.

R – Respond is the last stage of hearing.

Agent Takeaway:

> ➤ For the next week really focus on Active Listening to your prospects. Realize the information they give you, use it to sell them a home or market and follow up with them afterward.

TOP PRODUCER
SECRET #12

SCRIPTING

"When you script, you practice and when you practice, you perfect yourself; honing your sales skills and talent. Practice until you're naturally perfect!"

Shirleen Von Hoffmann

Scripting

Scripting can be one of the most important tools you can do as a New Home Salesperson. If you think that selling is just meeting some folks and talking them to death, hoping they will just buy a home from you, you are not an "EDGE Agent!" You might be lucky and sell a few but you will never be a top producer. "EDGE Agents" write down scripts, at least one to five for each sales situation, review and practice them every day. Rehearse them so much so they just roll off our tongue. As you practice on your buyers adjust them so they feel natural and easy.

Learn to play with your sales training and the more you practice the better and more successful you will be. Find some close lines that feel natural and not pressured. Have a choice of 4-5 to pick from so that when you have your potential, you can grab a close line that works for their personality. If the buyer shoots you down, try another one.

You should have scripts for all kinds of things...greetings, objections, prospecting, prequalifying, getting buyer information on a card, writing contracts, showing models, explaining processes, closing, you name it. It is important that your scripts are convincing and are natural. It is important that you practice them and keep the ones that work and feel natural in your repertoire. Any successful sales person will tell you that scripting is an important part of their sales process.

Many think having scripts is manipulating the sale. We think creating a script is part of being completely prepared.

Clients who hesitate in a selling situation can be saying that they need a few more facts to make them feel comfortable. The agent's job is to give them the data to help them make the decisions that are best for them. I view scripting as being able to help the client at the highest level, by accurately communicating in a convincing fashion the benefits of a particular decision.

To be well-scripted is to be prepared to help the client evaluate the situation carefully by weighing all sides less emotionally. The telephone solicitors, who sound as if they are reading from a cue card, are not well-scripted. An agent who is well-scripted can give an automatic response to a given situation he has been in before. He has practiced and prepared for the question before he gets the opportunity to answer it. Do people want to have a heart surgeon who is well-scripted? Sure, they do because it comes across as assurance, confidence and knowledge when it is done right.

To join the successful agents, you must learn to develop and deliver scripts with effectiveness. If you do, there will be no cap to your income. The different scripts will not change nor will the basic questions, problems, objections, and solutions. Once you learn to effectively cover these areas, you will be unstoppable. There are not many new objections created by buyers and sellers annually. If you have learned all the objections and can deliver your response to the objections well; you will be rewarded.

You may need to make modifications and practice them regularly, but you will not have to go through the process of learning 40 to 50 new scripts and dialogues. The difference between the amateur and the professional in all things in life is the skill and delivery. Tremendously skilled salespeople are well-scripted; you just cannot tell they are speaking from a script. Constant practice makes the difference.

Agent Takeaway: Practice Scripts Exercise

Your greeting script:

_____
_____
_____
_____

Getting a Card filled out:

_____
_____
_____
_____

Questions to find needs Script

_____
_____
_____
_____

Model Tour or Lot Script

_____
_____
_____

Lot Tour Script

_____
_____
_____
_____

Prequalification Script

_____

_____

_____

_____

Trial Close Script

_____

_____

_____

_____

Price Objection Script

_____

_____

_____

_____

Creating Urgency Script

_____

_____

_____

_____

Asking for the Sale Script

_____

_____

_____

_____

Reason for follow up Script

_____

_____

_____

_____

TOP PRODUCER
SECRET #13

OVERCOMING
OBJECTIONS

"You should be happy to get an objection, it says; "I am interested, tell me more about what I don't understand!"

Shirleen Von Hoffmann

Overcoming Objections

"I'm not interested at this time."
"I'm just too busy right now."
"Just fax me some info and I'll call you."
"We're just looking."
"I can get it cheaper somewhere else."
"I need to talk to my husband, wife, etc."
"I need to wait on this, or I need to think about it."
"We can't afford this price."
"Your price is too high."
"I am not sure; I'll get back to you."
"I am waiting for the right time to buy."
"What are your incentives? "
"The Builder down the street has more incentives."
Do any of these sound familiar?

If you are getting these, then you need to read on because an objection can actually be good news!

Objections = Opportunity

Most objections occur when a Sales Person has failed to;

· Build Value
· Build Rapport
· Build Trust
· Create a foundation
· Create urgency

Bad News

Some Sales Agents let the sale stop at an objection and never realize how easy it is to overcome objections.

They lose sales to competitors who know these skills.

Good News-If you are getting objections, that prospect is interested.

Once you learn how to overcome objections, those buyers can be your best allies.

Fact

Objections are a fact of life. They come with the territory if you are going to be in the Real Estate business.

The good news is there is a pattern you can follow with objections.

Fiction

Objections are not a stop sign.

They are a yield sign, telling you that you need more work and time with that prospect.

Listen carefully

When you <u>hear</u> an objection this is what you should <u>hear</u>...

"I am not sold on the facts and information you have thus far presented. Please give me more information, so that I might make a positive decision!"

Types of Objections-"The Four P's"

- ○ Price
- ○ Product
- ○ Personal
- ○ Postponement

Price

Price is a common objection.

When you have price as an objection it usually means you have missed building value in your product.

Example: "Your price is too high!"

Product

When you have product as an objection it usually means you have not built enough foundation on quality of construction, builder history, reputation, value vs. the competition.

Example: "I am going to look at some other builders' products and compare; I will get back to you."

Personal

When the objection is on a personal level whether that be with them or you, you need to spend more time developing rapport and relationship building with your prospect.

Example: "I'm not sure if my Husband will like this home, I'll have to check with him and get back to you."

Postponement

When the objection is in the form of postponement it could mean your prospect is not ready or afraid. "Buyers' remorse".

Spend more time building value and assuring them it's a great time to buy. Create Urgency.

Example: "We not sure if this is the right time to buy; we may wait and see what happens."

Agent Takeaway:

> ➢ We want you to really listen to objections and look at objections as opportunity.
> ➢ If you hear an objection, determine what is lacking in your routine.
> ➢ What do you need to do to further educate this prospect and get around the objection?

Ways to handle objections

Three skills that will help determine the validity of the objection.

Bypass It

Don't address it right away; see if it comes up again.

Take it Head On

Directly overcome at that moment.

Is it real?

Determine if it is a real objection by asking more questions.

Feel, Felt, Found

Zig Zigler always uses these terms when it comes to objections.

Feel, felt, found script example;

I see how you _feel_, others have _felt_ the same way too, until they _found_ out the equity they earned from getting such a great deal in the beginning!

Bring it up first

The best way to overcome objections is to know your objection and come up with a solution in advance.

Script a statement for each objection and practice it so you are ready!

Bring it up first script example:

"You know even though that lot size is not the biggest we have to offer in the community, it is actually a great deal because it is the closest to the golf course and the builder has priced it very aggressively to sell in 30 days!"

Agree

When faced with objections actively <u>listen</u> to them and agree so that you understand his point of view. Repeat his point of view back.

Agree Script Example:

<u>I agree</u>, the house may not have the biggest lot available, however the price is the lowest and it is the best buy you will find. In time getting the best price will pay off in the form of real dollars in your pocket!

Agent Takeaway:

> ➢ Pick an Objection that is challenging for you and a way to handle it.
> ➢ Your job will be to come up with a script for the objection practicing one of the techniques to handle an objection that we have given you.

TOP PRODUCER SECRET #14

NEGOTIATIONS

"Giving the price away is not real sales,
It's retail sales.
P. S. You're not in the retail sales business;
Retail Sales pays minimum wage!"

Shirleen Von Hoffmann

Negotiations

In a tough economy buyers are out and about making offers we would have never imagined in a seller's market. Having negotiation skills is mandatory in this market. When's the last time you brushed up on your skills? New markets require New Skills. You can't rely on old skills in a new market.

Even though Sales Agents may not be the final decision maker when it comes to a new home negotiation, you are at the core of a sale! You represent millions of dollars in inventory for your Builder. Your role is VERY important.

Your Builder relies on you to relay all of the credible information about the buyer and what they are looking for in the negotiation. With that fact in mind you must prepare with Negotiation skills as this market brings about some smart buyers with some crazy offers.

Win Win Strategies

You must be able to draw the fine line between getting the Builder what they need and the Buyer what he needs! When you build win-win strategies, you win too. Not always an easy task, especially in this market.

Creating win-win situations is at the core of powerful negotiations. Knowing all the skills of negotiations is an unconventional sales weapon and tactic that no successful sales person can live without, especially in this market. When you build win-win strategies you win too. Creating win-win situations is at the core of powerful negotiations.

7 Negotiation goals

1. To profit from the negotiations.
2. Learn all you can about the other side.
3. Find out where the bottom line is.
4. Study the other side.

5. Access the people on your side.
6. Find out what is fair and reasonable.
7. Know all the constraints of the deal.

7 Buyer tips for negotiating

1. They should be willing to negotiate.
2. Get them emotionally involved.
3. Never be the first to name your figure.
4. They always ask for more than they expect.
5. State that the final decision is not with you.
6. The other side will try to act uninterested.
7. Don't let the other person feel cheated.

Adapt like a chameleon

✓ Adapt your negotiating style to the negotiating environment. If the other side is quiet and controlled then you be quiet and controlled. Mimic your buyer.
✓ Probe to learn what the other side wants.
✓ Flush out weaknesses and uncover important information.

Psychology of negotiating

- Buyers always want what they can't have.
- Don't overwhelm the buyer with too many decisions.
- People have a fear of superiority in others.
- Everybody loves a Freebie.
- People trust that one good turn deserves another.
- Invoke the idea of the simple solution.
- *"Let's split the difference! "*
- *"Let's think outside the box."*
- Most people respond to the deadline.
- People practice the "Invested Time" Philosophy.

Agent Takeaway:

> ➤ We want you to study all of the strategies and try to start applying at least 50% on your current negotiations now. Apply the other 50% over the next few weeks.
> ➤ Pick your favorites and the ones that will be easy for you to remember and start using them right away.

Negotiation Success Factors

It is a proven statistic that **40%** of a negotiation is dependent on buyer motivation, **50%** is dependent on trust, while only **10%** is dependent on the structure of the deal. When you mix trust and rapport those numbers can go as high at 65%!

Those numbers are astounding! So if you don't think building rapport is important, you had better think again.

The goals of any negotiation

Trust

Trust is the cement of all good faith dealings between people. Create trust and you will become a successful negotiator.

Rapport

It is a proven fact that if not developed you will not be able to have an easy, successful negotiation.

Satisfaction

Both sides must get something they can live with and go away feeling satisfied.

Why Trust

The buyer will pay for a pound of friendship or a bucket of integrity if you deliver it.

Without trust the negotiation cannot proceed in a straightforward manner. If you can gain the other side's trust, you have a clear AdvantEdge over any competitor.

Negotiation timeline

If you build trust and rapport and sell yourself, your builder, your community, your product and its value you will have a very short, easy negotiation. When you don't establish a foundation you will have a much longer, harder negotiation.

Agent Takeaway:

> ➤ We want you to pay attention to developing trust and rapport with all buyers that you are negotiating with.
> ➤ Can you remember a negotiation scenario where you built trust and rapport? How easy was the negotiation?
> ➤ Can you remember a difficult negotiation? What was missing in the development of the relationship?

In order to know if you have a viable deal, you must know all aspects of a negotiation. Negotiation skills range from body language, to verbal clues, to developing trust, to listening skills to power words, to opening maneuvers to gaining the higher ground and of course how to keep the deal together. You need to be able to counter buyers who want rock bottom pricing and deals. Let's just talk about one item when it comes to negotiations.

Price:

A majority of prospects will not buy on price alone. The American retailers associations found that only 14 percent of consumers purchase solely on price. That means there is plenty of business out there where you don't have to be the lowest cost.

You will always have competitors whose prices may be lower. Then it's time to sell value, quality, location, delivery, reputation, service, support, terms and any other assets you have in your artillery. You must be ready for this objection and practice scripting over and over until you have a quick, natural response to individual pricing objections.

Here are just a few reasons why people will pay more...

- Knowledgeable sales force
- Trust
- Reputation
- Location
- Company stability
- Popularity
- Higher quality
- Scarcity
- Value
- Short delivery times
- Service
- Socially conscious companies
- Energy efficient items

- Long term savings
- Neighborhood amenities
- Financing options
- Included upgraded options

As the Salesperson you must always know your Builder's bottom line and your buyer's bottom line so you can structure a strategy that achieves a sale and everyone is happy. Active listening really helps achieve this task.

You may have to think about a few moves or counter offers that may occur, just as if you were playing a game of chess. You know the old saying, "Never show em your cards" Never let your Buyer know your Builder's bottom line or full incentives being offered. You can use those incentives to gain momentum on counter offers. Never print your incentives out on your pricing sheet or give them fully away when asked directly. When you practice these simple negotiating tactics, everyone involved in the deal, feels like they are getting what they need to get the deal done!

This is the time when Builders and Sales Agents need to make the most of every prospective buyer who walks through the door, overcoming pricing objections is one big way to gain the AdvantEdge over your competition.

TOP PRODUCER SECRET #15

FINANCE

"Finance will always be important in New Home Sales because
it's the biggest purchase of your buyer's life.
May I suggest, that to be the best;
Finance is a big part of your life too!"

Shirleen Von Hoffmann

Do you know financing?

So many agents talk too quickly and too much about lenders on site and hand off their buyers for prequalification, payments and things like that, way too soon. Want to scare off a potential buyer quickly? Give them a payment before they are ready. Those things are reality items and are negatives.

Right now, you want a "falling in love", process to occur. Instead let that buyer fall in love first...then slowly unfold the realities of purchase as they ask and as you probe you will know when the time is right to move to the next step. Think about it like buying a car. You want to drive the car and fall in love with it first. If they made you talk to the finance guy before you drove the car, you probably would never buy!

Finance and mortgages change daily, especially in this market. There is no way you, as a Sales Agent focusing on sales, can keep up with everything going on in the mortgage field. With that being said, you should know enough to get your mission accomplished as an Agent and move the buyer on to your Lender for detailed information. We want you to know enough to write the deal and once you have done that, move the buyers on to your lender.

What do you need to know?

Here are three crucial things to know and a way to achieve them.

You should know the top 10 popular loan programs available in the market.

When you meet with your lender to go over your open escrows, have them spend time with you explaining the details of the 10 most popular programs they use.

You should have a general idea of rates for those programs.

Have your Loan Officer fax you over rates for those programs weekly and enter those rates into your computer or keep them handy for reference.

You should know how to prequalify a buyer quickly

We have an easy program where you enter six details and you get a payment and ratios. Most Builder computer systems have some kind of prequalification program as well. We emphasize it should be EASY and FAST!

The goal is to get the prequalification done quickly and get back to your sale.

The goal is to know you are working with a good prospect and get back to your sale.

The goal is NOT to focus on financing unless the buyer wants you to focus on financing but instead focus on your home benefits, the sale and the close.

The goal is too NOT send that buyer away to be prequalified before you have written the sale or reserved the lot, if you can help it in any way.

There will be times when a buyer will have challenging credit that only a lender can work with and you will have to wait to write the deal.

Hopefully that will be a small percentage of the time. Remember if you are an Agent that cannot prequalify and you let that buyer walk out the door; an Agent who **can** prequalify will be writing that sale for that buyer at the next subdivision they visit.

You + Your Lender = Team

We recommend sitting down with your approved lender on a monthly basis and have them go over the most popular loans being used and the reasons why and the rates for those loans. Take one loan at a time and do your best to understand the aspects of those loans.

Rates, Points & Fees

Part of understanding finance is understanding rates for programs, fees for loans so you can explain them when needed.

Working as a team with your Lender and Title Company you can learn everything you need to know about Rates, Points and Fees.

Knowing Rates and Points

Rates change daily, sometimes more than once.

We recommend you have your lender send over the rates and points for the most popular programs on at least a weekly basis.

Enter these rates into your computer weekly for the most accurate payment calculations and fees to quote your customers.

There are many programs, too many for you to keep up with, thus the reason for only putting in the top 5 or most popular programs being used today.

Knowing Fees & Terms

We also recommend having your lender and title company go over a good Faith estimate in detail to fully explain to you all the fees they are charging your buyers and what they mean.

You should be able to do a brief explanation of fees and what they mean to your buyers when needed. It's important that they feel you are the expert in Real Estate and knowing enough about Finance to explain key items makes the "expert" come across.

Some fees you should know and be able to explain what they are for are; appraisal, credit, processing, underwriting, points, origination, tax service, recording, ALTA, CLTA, statement fees, impounds, recording fees, wire fees to name a few.

We are not saying you need to do the Lender's job or that you will always need to explain these items, but as a Real Estate Professional you should know what these fees mean and the approximate amount of these fees.

Agent Takeaway:

➤ We want you to have your lender & title company go over & explain what the fees mean on a good faith estimate, and how much the fees are. Write it down.

➤ Have the lender set up a routine of sending you rates and points each Friday.

➤ Enter 5 of the top programs into your computer for quick qualifications.

Buydowns

Buying the rate down is a great way to make the first years of living in a home affordable for the buyer.

Most lenders require the buyer to qualify at the note rate.

Seller can pay for buydowns out of the "allowable seller contributions".

How it works

A 3-2-1 buydown buys the interest down 3 points in year one, 2 points in year two and one point in year 3. Then the loan goes to the note rate for the remaining life of the loan.

Example: on a loan with a 6% note rate
1st year would be 3%
2nd year would be 4%
3rd year would be 5%
4th year would be 6% for the life of loan.

Basic Buydown Calculations

1-1 Factor is	.79 X Loan Amount
2-1 Factor is	2.31 X Loan Amount
3-2-1 Factor is	4.58 X Loan Amount

Factors will vary slightly by interest rate however these factors will give you a very good estimate of the buydown cost seller or buyer will incur.

Credit & FICO's

Fico scores rate the credit and give the lender a quick idea of the buyer's credit and the risk.

Usually there is one FICO score for each credit bureau pulled.

FICO is an acronym for Fair Isaac Corp.

Great Ficos range from 750-800+
Good Ficos range from 700-749
Acceptable Ficos range from 650-700
Poor Ficos range from 650 and below

The best questions you can ask your buyer is this;

> *"So tell me about your credit history, how is your credit.
> Do you know your Fico scores?"*

Then listen and watch for body language. If there is a lot of hesitation, get a credit report. If they say their credit is great, with confidence, it probably is!

Agent Takeaway:

> ➢ The buyer wants a 3-2-1 buydown on a $275,000.00 loan, what is the amount of the buydown.

Ratios

Once you have a payment PITI you divide it into the gross monthly income to get the top ratio. This is called the top ratio and should be somewhere around 30%.

Then take the payment PITI plus minimum monthly debt like credit cards, car payments, student loans and divide that number into gross income. This gives you the bottom ratio which should be somewhere around 40%.

Sometimes with compensating factors lenders will move these ratios slightly higher but this is a good rule of thumb.

TOP PRODUCER
SECRET #16

CLOSING

"Think of closing like steps on a path
that lead to a brook you gingerly step over.
When you make all the little steps of a sale properly, closing
doesn't feel like parting the Red Sea."

Shirleen Von Hoffmann

Closing

If you don't ask for the sale then you have done a lot of work for nothing. Closing the sale is one of the most important parts of your skills and it's your job. As you proceed with the sales process you should be doing room closes, plan closes, trial closes, site closes and closing in general. Always check the temperature of your prospect and listen for those buying signals. If you do this, then closing is but a brook to step over. If you don't do this then closing will be an ocean to cross.

Now you may have never learned these skills if you have not been in the market very long because in the previous market closing was easy. Most people were fighting over their lots and closing skills really didn't have to be used. In a tough market things are very different.

Closing Sales Psychology

The biggest obstacle for most salespeople is PSYCHOLOGICAL, not tactical. Most salespeople have subconscious beliefs, fears and expectations that prevent them from closing effectively. Unless the psychological issues are addressed, learning techniques won't help them

Self confidence is important. **The buyer will buy if you believe they will.** Make sure this is the only assumption you bring to work with you each morning.

Most sales people don't ask for the sale because they're afraid of rejection. Here's the deal. Don't take it personally. Here is what I know. If you have a psychological closing hang up, identify it and work through it. It's your job. Whatever you do, don't stop sales because of you and your thoughts, assumptions, pre-conceived notions or past experiences. Throw that all out!

Prospects make decisions on psychological levels

The psychology of customer decisions will play an important part in your sales and product marketing efforts. In addition to customer requirements, you will encounter important, but unspoken, customer feelings, bias, and politics.

Below are several specific unspoken psychological sales factors that have come to my attention. If you are upset about not closing a buyer, consider whether any of the following factors might apply to your situation.

Rapport : You must develop rapport or don't proceed with the sale or the close. Prospects will buy quicker from someone they like and trust.

Reputation: Especially now, when so many companies are going out of business, Reputation is important to consumers, especially on large purchases.

Trust: Can be as high as 60% of a sale.

Habit: A prospect makes decisions based on feelings that caused him the least amount of pain in the past and what might be familiar.

Time and Convenience: Sometimes prospects make buying decisions based on timing and ease. Delivering a product when a prospect needs it can be key to the sale. Making the process easy during these hectic times can be another huge selling factor, especially if they experienced a nightmare closing in the past.

Image: Having a great customer service reputation is very important when it comes to making the buying decision.

Branding: Your first job with a new prospect is to make your brand known. Does your prospect know your Builder? Many people want to know who is building their home and the history of the company or Builder.

Buyer's Remorse: can be overwhelming for buyers and sometimes they don't know why they are experiencing it. It usually stems from a panic state about a purchase so large. It's your job to recognize it and give the space around it.

Emotions: "Falling in Love"- Many people need to fall in love with a product and then they buy. This process can take time or can happen instantly. You will know by noticing them visualizing a lot, making plans in the future or talking about living there like they are. If you see this, it's a great sign!

Agent Takeaway:

> ➤ Identify your closing hang ups if any. Write them down along with a plan of how you will rid yourself of them.

Closing Types

In new home sales there are the normal closes, mini closes, trial closes, room closes, plan closes, and site closes. Just for grins I thought I would include a bunch of different closing ideas for you to play with and see if you can use them as well in your Sales Routine.

Affordable Close - ensuring people can afford what you are selling.

Alternative Close - offering a limited set of choices.

Assumptive Close - acting as if they are ready to decide.

Balance-sheet Close - adding up the pros and the cons.

Best-time Close - emphasize how now is the best time to buy.

Bonus Close – offer from seller to clinch the deal

Concession Close - give them a concession in exchange for the close.

Conditional Close - link closure to resolving objections.

Cost of Ownership Close - compare cost over time with competitors.

Daily Cost Close - reduce cost to daily amount.

Demonstration Close - show them the goods.

Economic Close - help them pay less for what they get.

Embarrassment Close - make *not* buying embarrassing.

Emotion Close - trigger identified emotions.

Empathy Close - empathize with them, then sell to your new friend.

Extra Information Close - give them more info to tip them into closing

Future Close - close on a future date.

Give-Take Close - give something, then take it away.

Humor Close - relax them with humor.

Hurry Close - go fast to stop them thinking too much.

Minor points Close - close first on the small things.

Never-the-best-time Close - for customers who are delaying.

No-hassle Close - make it as easy as possible.

Now-or-never Close - to hurry things up.

Opportunity Cost Close - show cost of not buying.

Ownership Close - act as if they own what you are selling.

Price-promise Close - promise to meet any other price.

Puppy Close - acting cute to invoke sympathy and a nurturing response.

Quality Close - sell on quality, not on price.

Rational Close - use logic and reason.

Repetition Close - repeat a closing action several times.

Retrial Close - go back to square one.

Reversal Close - act as if you do not want them to buy the product.

Shopping List Close - tick off list of their needs.

Similarity Close - bond them to a person in a story.

Standing-room-only Close - show how others are standing in line to buy.

Summary Close - tell them all the things they are going to receive.

Testimonial Close - use a happy customer to convince the new customer.

Think About It Close - give them time to think about it.

Treat Close - persuade them to 'give themselves a treat'.

Valuable Customer Close - offer them a special 'valued customer' deal.

Ultimatum Close - show negative consequences of not buying.

Yes Close - get them saying 'yes' and they'll keep saying 'yes'.

Agent Takeaway:

> ➢ Try a new close every other day from the list we have provided.
> ➢ Pick 10 of your favorites and use them on a regular basis.

"Closing can be a lot like fly fishing. If you tug hard on the line, it will snap and the fish will get away. The best method is a gentle coaxing that gradually brings the fish in to shore - although sometimes when they are spooked you have to let them out again and calm them down further away."

5 Sales Closing Tips

There are many closing techniques and there are some common tips that are offered to make closing even more successful.

ABC

ABC is a common term which stands for 'Always Be Closing', which is both good and bad advice. ABC is good advice when it is used to keep in mind that you are always aiming towards a close. It is bad when you just use it to mean battering the customer to death with a barrage of unsubtle closing techniques.

When you have used a closing technique, be quiet afterwards and let them respond.

Silence is Golden

Silence also builds <u>tension</u> and can work for you in a couple of ways. It will give them the opportunity to tell you how they are feeling about the property and the purchase, so make sure to use active listening. Also it will encourage them to respond - and a response to a well-put closing question will hopefully be positive. Again, if you have not built rapport, silence may be awkward.

Watch emotions

Watch out for the other person not only in what they say but also in the <u>emotions</u> behind the words. You can sell on emotions, close on emotions and also stop the sales based on emotions. Never try closing when they are in a negative emotional state - you will only cause further objection.

Over-closing

It is not unknown for sales people to talk their customers into closure then carry right on and talk them out again. It is often the fear of the other person saying 'no' that often causes a sales person to keep on talking. You must have faith and also accept that when they say 'no' it is no real comment about you.

Closing need not mean a sale today

Unlike some sales, in new home Sales, there are "bebacks." When talking about the biggest purchase of someone's life it may require that the sales person follow up aggressively to set up a follow up meeting.

When you meet the customer again, then you can have intermediate goals and closure may just be an agreement to meet again. Generally, if you are getting the other person to commit to some action, you are moving the sale forward.

In all of these methods, remember that all closing techniques are appropriate only in particular circumstances. By using relationship selling methods, seeking to understand them and meet their needs, both professional and human, the close should be relatively easy.

Remember; people aren't interested in what you have to sell, they are interested in what they want and need. Sell them what they want and need.

NEVER FORGET...ASK FOR THE SALE

Never forget the sale belongs to the closer. No matter which way you choose to do it, you must Ask for the Sale!

Prospects love to buy what they need and to buy what they need you must find out what those needs are, sell them those needs and close the deal.

Taking into consideration you have been trial closing along the way and customer sales psychology, excessive and repeated use of sales closes may permanently alienate your prospect. However you don't want to forget to Ask for the Sale. Many Sales People get so involved with the fancy stuff they forget the basics like, "Asking for the Sale".

Again some Sales People don't ask for the Sale in fear they are going to get a "NO' which they take as rejection. Don't fall into this trap as it can turn into a fear or avoidance issue. Being in Sales doesn't really allow time for fears, shyness or taking things personally.

With the assumption that you are asking great questions, listening, providing great solutions and checking the pulse by trial closing, my philosophy is to use one sales closing technique during any single meeting or phone conversation. Using too many closes in one meeting is a typical mistake; but, not using any is another mistake. Using one close during a meeting will help to move a deal forward. Using two closes may be helpful in very few cases. But, using three or more seems very risky to me.

In closing, I like to use more of a conversational close, not a scripted close. It's more natural and comes across better to the prospect.

There are some prospects who want to be asked for their order. If they seem to be this type, if they look interested, and if the time is right, then simply ask for the order? If they say "NO", then you know that you still have work to do with that prospect.

Here's an easy way to ask for the sale;

"Mr. Smith we have discussed all of your home buying needs and this home seems to meet those needs. During this time we have settled all of your concerns and shown that my company can meet all of your requirements. So unless there is anything I am missing, let's take this home off the market and put your name on it today!"

Agent Takeaway:

> ➤ Never again let an interested prospect leave your office without asking for the sale.
> ➤ Come up with a few scripts to use that feel comfortable and use them.

TOP PRODUCER
SECRET #17

SALES CIRCLES

"Doctors, Lawyers and all business people
have a process to follow that reminds
them of their perfection and order.
It makes you more efficient,
so things don't get missed."

Shirleen Von Hoffmann

Do you have a sales circle?

A sales circle is the process or cycle you go through with a client to sell or close a sale. If you are good at what you do, you probably know what a sales circle is and you have a few of them.

A new home sales person should have a couple of sales circles. The first one would be to sell the home and close. The second one would be writing a contract. They should be looked at separately. Your scripting will come into play inside of your sales circles.

This is such an important step in being a great sales person we are going to take some time and ask you to tell us your current sales circle for each process. You have two blank sales circles; let's take some time to fill in what your current process for selling a home and writing the contract.

Sales Circle #1 (The sale)

- ○ You should have a meet and greet
- ○ Building Rapport
- ○ An explanation of your products you have
- ○ Asking questions to find needs.
- ○ What are they needing (active listening)
- ○ Walking through and viewing the product.
- ○ Answering questions.
- ○ Help them visualize themselves in your home.
- ○ Talking up the community and the Builder.
- ○ The benefits of living there, schools, parks, shopping, golf...
- ○ Options included in the price.
- ○ Options they can add.
- ○ Overcoming any obstacles they may have.
- ○ Prequalifying them.
- ○ Trial closing and closing

Contract Sales Circle

Having a purchase contract circle is important for many reasons. You should follow a pattern when you write contracts just like you do when you are trying to sell a home. Again, when you follow a pattern, you are less likely to miss steps.

When you sign a contract with a client it is easy to get "off course". The client is asking questions and interrupting and before you know it you get off track, forget a step, or miss explaining an important item. If you have a cycle in place, that you follow you will be able to fall right back in line and not miss a beat.

Taking control of the sale is one way to avoid getting off track. When the client asks you questions that you know you will be covering, just simply tell them that. Something like, "You know we are going to cover that when we get to the_____part of this contract." This sort of leadership keeps you in charge and in control of the contract. It's that simple.

You should go through your entire contract and any addendums or attachments and be able to explain pertinent items to the clients in one or two sentences. It's your responsibility as a real estate professional to know what all of your forms mean, every paragraph. And you should be able to explain it briefly and easily.

Allow them the time to read what they wish. The script for this may be like this, *"I am going to give you a brief explanation of important items in the contract. However, I want you to know you are welcome and should read the entire contract yourself. If you come up with any additional questions I am happy to answer them anytime."*

Sales Circle #2 (The close) should have these steps.

- o An agreement of what the buyer is purchasing i.e. which lot, legal description
- o Address

- ○ Going over Colors of home
- ○ Going over Roof color
- ○ Going over Elevation
- ○ Going over Options included
- ○ Going over Options they will pick
- ○ CC & R specifics
- ○ Estimated completion date, how that can move and why.
- ○ Writing the contract
- ○ Explaining everything in the contract
- ○ Explaining the escrow process
- ○ The construction process
- ○ The loan process and timelines for prequalification, approval and close.
- ○ Timelines for picking options and what deposits will be required at that time.
- ○ Deposits due today and any to follow, what they are for, what is refundable with a cancellation.
- ○ Locking in the rate safely to accommodate a completed construction date.
- ○ Obtaining homeowners insurance
- ○ Who the title company is and what they do
- ○ Explaining warranty procedures and timeframes
- ○ Builder's walk through procedure explanations
- ○ Appliance explanations and warranties

The more thorough you are with your sales circles, the more you lead the sale and have fewer interruptions from the buyer asking questions that will make your sales flow go off track. Remember the buyers are looking to you to lead them through this process.

When you start your sales circle you can start with an opening statement like, "We are going to cover a lot of things today and I do go over every step of the process so... I am going to ask you to write down your questions as we go, and I will answer any unanswered questions at the end of our meeting. I will hopefully cover everything so you won't have any unanswered questions."

And most likely you will have no questions left unanswered if you have a good sales circle. The more you cover in your sales circles the more "in the know" the buyer is which results in fewer phone calls during the process, fewer complaints for the builder and for you. There is nothing worse than when a buyer says, "You didn't explain this and that to me."

When you follow a sales circle EVERYTIME, you will cover everything in a manageable timeframe, it will become a standard and you won't miss or forget items. You will have a much easier escrow and happier buyer for the ultimate finale. And let's face it, we all love a great finale to a sale which will bring a referral to friends and family.

Sales Circle #1 Sale Example

Prospect Sales Circle

Follow up or Follow Through → Meet & Greet → Model Walk → Summary Narrowing in on product → Closing → Follow up or Follow Through

Sales Circle #2 Contract Example

Contract Sales Circle

Closing → Property Details → Contract Details → Procedures of Sales → Questions → Closing

Agent Takeaway:

> ➤ We want you to come up with two Sales circles.
> ➤ Take your time and really come up with complete sales circles that cover all aspects of a sale and of writing a contract.
> ➤ Keep the sales circles close by and follow them for the next few months trying to perfect your cycles and not miss one step in a sale.

EDGE AGENT SECRET #18

GOT THE SALE – NOW WHAT?

"If 90% of the world's problems are poor communications,
then work really hard to
make sure you are in the other 10%!"

Shirleen Von Hoffmann

Tracking and Follow up

Tracking your sales is very important because you need to be on top of everything going on with your buyer. You also answer to the Builder on every sale so knowing every detail is an important part of your job.

At least once a week you should be tracking your loans in process.

At least once a week you should be tracking your escrows in process.

At least once a week you should be meeting with your superintendent on your homes in process and completion dates.

Once you have new estimated completion dates from your superintendent you should be notifying your buyers and your lenders.

At least once a week you should be walking your homes to make sure mistakes are not occurring with options, flooring...While you are in the homes you can take digital pictures and email them to your buyers.

At least once a week you should be relaying pertinent information to your Sales Manager via Sales Meetings on the progress of your sales in escrow.

Escrow Tracking Report

You should have an escrow tracking report that covers every stage of the process. This report should have; Lot, name, completion date, choosing options date. Loan in process and approved date, interest rate lock in date and expiration date and various construction stages dates. This report is a must if you want to stay on top of your escrows. When you have numerous escrows going at the same time, you will never be able to keep track of all of the details unless you have a report like this.

Keeping the sale

Sometimes it's very hard to keep a sale in escrow for six months. You have a lot of work to do even after you have a sale. You may battle issues like completion timing, pricing challenges, options add ons that are too late, loan issues, buyer's remorse and a number of other obstacles. The sale is done when the deal is closed, in the meantime you have work to do.

Think of the "in between time" as a time to make your buyers part of your family. You should keep them informed, on track, warm and cozy. You should anticipate their needs and you should be on your game.

You should have a routine with your buyers that keeps them informed, in the loop, in the know and ahead of schedule. There are numerous things they are going through and need to be doing and your reminding them of these things not only makes you "The expert" but makes you "The Hero" and the "End All".

So you have a buyer; that means you have a person who is pretty stressed out because they are making the biggest purchase of their lifetime. They also may be confused and overwhelmed by the experience.

The more you keep them informed and on task, the fewer problems you will have in escrow. Never forget ninety percent of the problems are due to poor communications.

You should have a routine where you keep them informed once a week about the progress of their home.

You should have knowledge of their loan process and be able to work with the lender to stay on top of those details for them.

You should have a lot of different marketing material you can send them once a month that keeps them reminded of items they need to tackle. Inform them on the process.

Here are some examples of things you can be sending them;

- Tips on not packing their important paperwork that might be needed for the loan like bank statements, taxes, W-2', paystubs...
- Locking in their interest rates making sure they check with you first for completion timing.
- Obtaining hazard insurance quotes in advance and knowing who they are using.
- Moving tips and a moving guide.
- Tips for selling their home.
- A step by step flyer on setting up their new utilities, mailbox keys...
- A step by step flyer on the loan process.
- A step by step flyer on the process of being in escrow and everything you need them to do.
- A step by step flyer on closing and what they will need to do to close, all the way down to getting a cashier's check and timing from signing to funding.

Agent Takeaway:

> ➢ Have marketing materials prepared that you can send out to your buyers to keep them informed about the process. Commit to it.
> ➢ Come up with an escrow tracking form that is yours alone to keep you organized and on top of every escrow.

TOP PRODUCER SECRET #19

THE FINALE

"Finally the finale, now the real work starts, stay on task until the final is filed and the file is in the closed, Happy-buyer-referral drawer! Then take your bow!"

Shirleen Von Hoffmann

The Finale

The Finish of the sale is everything. It is what your buyer will remember most. It is what will get you referrals and build clients for life.

So many escrows end up with unhappy buyers because of last minute mistakes because everyone rushes to a finish line. Remember your buyers are trying to plan their lives and won't have much patience for last minute snafus! It's really up to you to keep your cool, keep the sale organized and going in the right direction until the keys are handed out and your buyers are happily living in their home.

It's very important in the last week that you are communicating on every level, at every stage and that you are ahead, instead of possibly behind the ball. There is nothing worse than having a moving truck full of a buyer's life, outside your sales office and not able to let them move in because the Lender didn't fund or the final isn't done or the insurance wasn't received or something wasn't installed right.

Mistakes happen, miscommunications happen but do your best to communicate on all levels and you will avoid most common mistakes. And if you follow everything we have talked about thus far, your chances for misunderstandings, miscommunications will fall to a very low percentage.

Warranties

A positive buyer experience also rests on a good warranty program, with quick response times and easy procedures for obtaining the fixes. You can have a perfectly smooth escrow and get your bad rap from the warranty department.

Know your warranties procedures and people inside and out. Again explaining the process to your buyers is very important.

Letting the buyer know you are a one stop shop and if there are any complications or questions about warranty they can contact you. That way you stay in the loop if you receive complaints about the warranty department.

You have invested a lot of time and energy into your buyers and their experience. You want to make sure their experience stays positive all the way to closing. It should be your top priority to have a smooth finish and a grand finale!

Partners in Success

Make sure you take the time to thank your partners for success who helped you get this far and close another happy buyer. Title Companies, Realtors, Lenders and even your Superintendent all play critical roles in your Finale. When they do a great job, you should make it a point to recognize their efforts with a "Thanks, for a job well done", call or card. Many times their hard work goes unnoticed and unappreciated.

Agent Takeaway:

> ➤ We want you to make sure you put in your sales circle a time to fully explain the warranty process to your buyers.
> ➤ We want you to come up with a flyer you can give them which has all the pertinent numbers to call and restates the warranty procedures to make it very easy for them to take care of warranty items. They will forget much of the details towards the finale so they will appreciate your helping them to remember these details.

TOP PRODUCER SECRET #20

FOLLOW UP

"If you are not following up with your happy buyers for referrals, then you wasted a lot of time, energy and money to create happy buyers."

Shirleen Von Hoffmann

Staying in Touch

Stay in touch with your buyers once they are closed. Now they ARE a part of your family and hopefully you had a great experience with them. When you stay in touch, it shows them you care about them and that your relationship goes beyond a sale.

Never forget a happy buyer can be your best sales asset. You can feel free to tell your prospects to walk the neighborhood and ask your home owners how much they like living there. If you and your Builder have done your job, your homeowners will sell for you.

Asking for a referral

So you have put in all this work to make your buyer happy, well adjusted into their new home and part of your family. Why do you go through all of this work?

So you can ask for a referral of course!

So many Agents make the mistake of closing the sale and moving on. Remember all of your buyers have friends and family who will be coming to see their new home. And most friends and families love living close to each other.

We will restate this fact:

The cost to obtain a new buyer is 10-20 times more than to get referrals from buyers you already have.

Think about that fact. An even more important fact is that it will be a very warm lead verses a cold lead. This will make your life so much easier.

Always have a referral program you can tell your buyers about. Ask them to refer you to their family and friends. It's the easiest kind of sales call, a warm one. And if you did a great job for them, it will be a much cheaper way of obtaining a buyer than from scratch.

And one more thing, don't stop marketing to your past clients after a couple of attempts. People's lives are always changing, everyday. Don't forget that you worked hard to make a client for life. So have a marketing plan in place that markets to them for life.

Happy Sales!

Agent Takeaway:

> ➤ Have a marketing plan for your buyers who have closed. It must be a lifelong marketing plan touching them quarterly and semi annually.
> ➤ Finally, have at least three separate ways you ask for a referral from each one of your buyers. Ask every time!

Chapter 4

SERVICES WE PROVIDE

SALES TRAINING TO GO!

TOP PRODUCER SECRETS ONLINE

Our clients can purchase one full year (52 weeks) worth of Sales Training for their weekly sales meetings.

There is nothing like LIVE training to get a meeting going. We provide the online LIVE training, the topics, the power points, the agent hand outs and the agent takeaways. You and Your Agents learn via live webinars. All you need to do is call a meeting, all the work and training is done for you!

Topics include

1. Meet & Greet; ways to make them remember you and your community
2. How to walk the models; the easy way!
3. Building rapport; starts with good open ended questions?
4. Easy ways to market; you and your Builder
5. Moving fence sitters and Contingencies
6. Follow Up
7. Overcoming Objections
8. The Top Performer's Habits
9. Understanding financing and prequalification
10. Powerful Negotiations
11. Closing Techniques…Asking for the Sale
12. Got the Sale…Now What?U

Hcall us at (866)600-EDGE to schedule

SALES TRAINING TO GO!

TOP PRODUCER SECRETS CD'S

Our clients can purchase 12 months worth of Sales Training for their weekly sales meetings.

On each monthly CD, we provide the topics, the power points, the agent hand outs and the agent takeaways. You simply teach it. Anyone can teach it, a trainer, a sales manager or a senior sales agent. All the work is done for you! When you hire new agents, no problem, have them study the CD's!

Topics include

1. Meet & Greet; ways to make them remember you and your community
2. How to walk the models; the easy way!
3. Building rapport; starts with good open ended questions?
4. Easy ways to market; you and your Builder
5. Moving fence sitters and Contingencies
6. Follow Up
7. Overcoming Objections
8. The Top Performer's Habits
9. Understanding financing and prequalification
10. Powerful Negotiations
11. Closing Techniques...Asking for the Sale
12. Got the Sale...Now What?

Order at www.homebuildersadvantedge.com

EDGE AGENT MASTERS CERTIFICATION

For Agents who want to further their sales skills to a whole new level we offer our Edge Agent Mastery Course. In this certification you will receive the following:

A Master Edge Agent will obtain;

- 8 weeks self study certification.
- Weekly 1 on 1 coaching with a Master Sales Coach
- 12 monthly 1 hour conference calls with other students and master trainers to discuss goals, situations, challenges and objectives.
- Master Edge Agent Certificate

HOURLY CONSULTING

At Home Builders AdvantEdge we can provide solutions to your needs on an hourly basis.

· Sales Training and Coaching

We can formulate a package to fit your Sales training needs, on an hourly basis.

· Sales and Marketing Ideas

We can work with your marketing and advertising department to come up with innovative ideas to help you sell in this market.

· Mortgage Company issues

When you are having issues with your mortgage company and cannot figure out why, we have the knowledge to go inside and work through the problems with viable solutions.

· Communication & Client follow up Systems

We have communication and client follow up packages we offer to our homebuilders.   We can train your employees and sales agents how to use these systems on an hourly basis

SALES TRAINING

At Home Builders AdvantEdge we pride ourselves on the fact that will come in and train your Sales Agents, on site, one on one.

We have many different packages for Home Builder's to choose from according to the needs and wants of the Builder.

"Foundation" 8 Hour private group training

This training is done in your meeting room and is an all day intensive sales training on the needs of your group and edge agent skills and techniques

"Frame"3 Day on site 1 on 1 Sales Agent training

This sales training is done one on one at the community, where we have time to really focus on the needs of the agent and teach those needs along with edge agent skills. We summarize the overall quality of the agent, strengths and weaknesses via a report card to the builder at the completion of the training.

"Finish" 2 Day Edge Agent Certification-in house

Private, in house, intensive training with all of your sales agents teaching them the edge agent skills necessary to become "certified" edge agents. Two coaches will be instructing this course which will be on your premises for two full days. Edge Agent certification includes monthly follow up conference calls with your agents for a total of six months.

SEMINARS

At Home Builders AdvantEdge our Seminars speak directly to New Home Sales Professionals and the skills they will require to sell in this market.

We have many different packages for Home Builder's to choose from according the needs and wants of the Builder.

· "1st Walk" - 1/2 Hour Sales meeting

We come into your weekly Sales Meeting and speak to your agents to begin the process of teaching them to think like an edge agent.

· "2nd Walk" - 4 Hour in house seminar

In this seminar we come to your office meeting room and provide your agents with a four hour course on edge agent tactics, ideas and habits. In this meeting we will have time to speak about facts of the market, changing the way they think and actually practice some edge agent techniques with them.

· "Final" - All day in house Seminar

In this Seminar we will have more time to go through our entire seminar and work with your agents in a group setting on all of the things they will need to start practicing Edge Agent skills.

SECRET SHOPPING

All successful companies utilize Secret Shopping to monitor and perfect sales performance.

Do you **really** know how your agents are performing? Are they doing as much as they can to close the client? You pay a lot to walk one client through the door – are your agents just letting them walk away?

HBA uses a hidden pinhole camera to record a normal client's interaction with your sales agent. There is no better way to see how your Agent's are coming across to your prospects. Using this information, you can improve your customer experience and convert more leads. Our trained shoppers use the latest technology to capture the experience that your customers get when approaching your business.

Let HBA shop your sales agents and see a clear, no-nonsense evaluation of their performance. HBA has the expertise to help your agents improve their sales techniques and convert more leads.

Our shops include:

1. **DVDs** – Get two DVDs containing pristine audio and video of our secret shopper's interaction with your agent.
2. **Written Report** – Comprehensive, clear cut, detailed evaluation of your Salesperson shop, including HBA's ten core competencies.
3. **HBA Senior Management Review** – At HBA we have over twenty five years in new homes sales experience. In the shop

report review process, our Senior Management not only does many of our shops but they also review every shop and provide you with a breakdown of training suggestions and areas for improvement.

4. **Agent Follow up Tracking** - Are your agents following up with their customers? Find out if they called our secret shopper for three weeks after our visit.

5. **Quick Turnaround** – Get your results quickly – in most cases, 5-10 business days.

We also offer:

- **Agent Secret Shops & Follow up Coaching**
  Internet Shop
- **Phone Shop**
- **Audio Shop**
- **Mini Shop**
- **Competition Shop**
- **Lender Shops**
  Video & Report Shop, Phone Shop, Internet Shop
- **Design Center**
  Video & Report Shop, Phone Shop

BUILDER BUNDLE

At Home Builders AdvantEdge we have so many options to help you become successful in this market.

In the builder bundle you get every option we have to offer and more!

- One on one Sales Training at your community
- Edge Agent Certification
- Six month follow up with your agents & managers
- Communication package
- Client Follow up package
- Prequalification tools
- One on one sales agent coaching and follow up
- Follow up courtesy shops
- Agent report cards

ABOUT THE AUTHOR

Shirleen Von Hoffmann is President & Sales Coach of HBA-Home Builder's AdvantEdge. HBA is an innovative sales coaching company that teaches New Home Agents techniques that elevate them to a fresh place of success. We are a National Company that specializes in Sales Agent Secret Shopping, Sales Coaching, Seminars, and One-on-One onsite training for New Home Builder's.

In her twenty eight year career Shirleen has only focused in New Home Sales. Shirleen is an accomplished Sales Coach, Inspirational Speaker and Author. As a past Top Producer and Manager in new

home sales and finance, she has closed well over one billion in new home sales over the years. She is tenacious, to the point and speaks in a sales language that her followers love!

She believes the time has come to take our New Home Sales Agents to a new and different level of selling. Once they achieve this echelon of their training they are more responsible for their sales and those extra sales efforts make a direct difference for the Builder's bottom line.

"My passion and focus is working with Builders and Agents to give them better solutions to achieve more sales. Through video we can evaluate sales performance and coach out the changes that need to take place. Agents are taught to do the extra steps necessary to be the very best! This means a lot of time spent on the prospect experience, model and lot tours, aggressive marketing strategies and consistent follow up with prospects.

I get personally involved with every Builder and Agent that I work with. I am not your ordinary Speaker or Trainer; I roll up my sleeves and work with your sales teams to make them the best they can be. It doesn't matter how long it takes, as long as when I leave they are the best they can be! I insist on perfecting their selling techniques through coaching, mentoring, takeaways, scripting and role play. I teach them in a way that most Sales People learn best, in their language, giving them relative, useful information that they can take away and mix into their repertoire. My passion for what I do comes through as better sales performance for you! I love to share my wealth of knowledge and simplistic sales wisdom with those who wish to achieve higher thresholds of sales and prosperity."

Shirleen resides in Northern California and spends the majority of her week motivating and working with Sales Teams one on one, to perfect their skills and enlighten them to a new way of selling.

In her spare time Shirleen runs a non-profit "Calling all Angels" a foundation that feeds and supports Cancer Patients in need.
www.callingallangels.us
www.journeyhomebook.com

You can read her articles in many new home trades' publications including, Ideas Sales and Marketing Magazine and Sales and Marketing Online from the NAHB National Association of Home Builder's. You can learn more by visiting:

Site www.homebuildersadvantedge.com
Blog www.thequeenofsales.com

In closing;

We look forward to meeting you and helping you with your career very soon. In the meantime here is our contact information if there are any questions we can answer.

Shirleen Von Hoffmann, President & Sales Coach
Homebuilders AdvantEdge
10100 Fair Oaks Blvd #E
Fair Oaks, CA 95628
866 600-EDGE   Direct
916 880-5666   Fax
www.homebuildersadvantedge.com
info@homebuildersadvantedge.com

LaVergne, TN USA
13 October 2010
200630LV00003B/209/P